England
Never Slept

England
Never Slept

A Boy's Remembrances
of World War II

John Hignett

Library of Congress Control Number:		2010918248
ISBN:	Hardcover	978-1-4568-3063-2
	Softcover	978-1-4568-3062-5
	Ebook	978-1-4568-3064-9

To order additional copies of this book, contact:
Xlibris Corporation
1-888-795-4274
www.Xlibris.com
Orders@Xlibris.com
90232

CONTENTS

Chapter 1

BLITZ

The front door of my grandfather's terraced house left its hinges and flew into the road, taking GranDad with it. A violet-blue flash, followed by bright yellows and reds, lit the midevening sky. A deafening roar followed as the ground trembled and the houses shook. Glass fell, and roof tiles crashed onto the road.

That was my first recollection of London's blitz in early September 1940.

Minutes before, GranDad sat me on the low wall to the right of the door while he went back inside to get something he'd forgotten. All I had to do was obey his orders, and I'd grown used to that, as almost every night, the wailing of air-raid sirens sounded their warning message, and we left the house for the refuge of the shelters built in blocks at the end of the road. That night GranDad, not my mother, woke me and told me to come quickly, throwing his Home Guard jacket—one I wore when I played soldiers—over my shoulders.

I sat by the door, waiting for him to reappear, and then watched—as if in slow motion—as he flew through the air, clutching my slippers. The brass doorknocker detached and smashed into the windows across the road. They collapsed and showered down.

After a silence—or perhaps I'd closed out the noise—I heard water gushing from loft tanks and water pipes, falling glass and roof tiles, people's voices, some shouting, some shrieking, and babies crying. I couldn't tell where the voices came from nor could I see GranDad because a thick swirl of dust and acrid smoke engulfed the area and made my eyes water. I wiped my eyes with the back of my hands.

As the dust and smoke cleared, I saw a figure running toward GranDad, who lay in the road. Another man swooped me up and carried me to the shelter. I threw up an arm to protect my head as we ducked into the narrow entrance between the blast wall and the shelter entrance. A heavy dark green curtain covered the doorway. The man dumped me on the bottom of tiered bunk beds that lined the shelter walls. His stern but friendly voice told me to stay put, and then he left.

The shelter, ten feet wide and fifty feet long, was poorly lit with smoky oil lamps. I'd watched them being built—solid brick walls and a reinforced flat slab concrete roof covered in pitch or tar—on the side of the road, giving limited access through the road. A brick blast wall, two bricks thick, same as the walls, covered three feet either side of the doorway.

A torchlight moved toward me down the centre passageway. I made out a lady's silhouette. She asked me if I was all right and if I knew where my mother was. I remembered her. She and my mother talked on nights we sat waiting for the all clear siren. I told her that Mother had left two days earlier to take my younger sister to a safer place in the country and I was to follow shortly. When she asked about GranDad, I blurted out what I'd seen and then released a flood of tears. That first sign of emotion wasn't for myself but for the unknown and the fear of what might have happened to him. For the first time in my life, I felt completely alone.

The lady told me everything would be all right, but she didn't sound convincing. I told her my name was John, the same as GranDad's, and I was six and three-quarters years old. She smiled and told me I was a big boy for my age and "big boys don't cry," so I wiped my tears on GranDad's jacket sleeve.

Nothing I experienced later in life reached the depths of despair I felt at that moment, and I found it difficult to cry again.

The blackout curtain parted, and the man who'd brought me to the shelter came inside supporting GranDad. They were cursing, some words I'd heard before and some I hadn't, but I knew I wasn't allowed to use them. GranDad hushed when he saw me.

"Thank God!" GranDad said as he tousled my curly brown hair. "Take more than bloody Hitler to knock us out, won't it, John?"

GranDad turned to ask the man for news of our street and the area. A terraced house behind my grandfather's had a direct bomb hit, two houses farther down had been hit, and the church at the top of the road had been hit too. There was no news of casualties yet, the man told GranDad, but he feared the worst.

GranDad closed his eyes. When he opened them, he rubbed the back of his head. There was blood on his hand. His face was grazed and bleeding down one side. Part of his jacket sleeve was missing. He insisted he was all right, but the lady who'd spoken to me told him to sit. He sat on the bunk opposite me, muttering about not making a fuss and others were worse off. She didn't let him put her off.

He cursed as she dabbed iodine on his head. I'd this treatment for cuts and grazes and felt for GranDad. I'd been told that if it didn't sting, it wouldn't do any good. I was old enough to know that everything that was good for me either tasted awful or caused physical or emotional pain. Grown-ups seemed to know what was good or bad without any explanation except "It's good for you."

An air-raid warden I'd seen before came through the entrance. His job, as my mother had explained to me, was to coordinate warnings, check the blackout curtains on windows, and assist in helping people who were bombed out.

GranDad's manned a searchlight at night, looking for bombers in the sky. Alongside him were gunners of what everyone called ack-ack guns, named because of the sound they made. I grew used to hearing those sounds. There were drums of wire rope whose ends were fitted with grey cigar-shaped barrage balloons with three distinct fins hanging like Dumbos in the sky. Barrage balloons discouraged bombers from flying too low for accurate bombing. GranDad commented that if the gunners were half as good at shooting down bomber planes as they were barrage balloons, there would be no problem. True or false, I never knew with GranDad. Even today, I still quiver when I see similar balloons flying over sports arenas.

"Why was the air-raid warning so bloody late tonight?" GranDad growled to the warden.

"Don't know, John," the warden relied. "By the pasting London's getting tonight, it's a wonder anything is working. There are fires all over."

GranDad accepted the warden's explanation and nodded.

"Any local news?" the man asked.

The warden said several houses had been hit, two had families inside, and there were people in the church. How many dead or injured he didn't know. He shook his head. "There's going to be quite a few. Let's pray for heavy cloud cover tomorrow. The first clear evening this week, and look at the mess those bombers made."

Two people, both shaken up from a narrow escape, came into the shelter. Grandpa told me to lie on my bunk and sleep. I'd just closed my eyes when the ground shook and the shelter trembled. "Christ!" and "Shit!" and other expletives came out from all around. Even though it wasn't a night for sleeping, tiredness crept up on me, and I dozed off.

When I woke, the sun shone through the shelter entrance door. Noises from outside, particularly tin cups clinking, attracted my attention. The shelter was nearly empty. GranDad was nowhere to be seen. I got up, put on my slippers, and walked into the bright sunlight, blinking as my eyes adjusted to the bright light.

On the pavement, two Salvation Army ladies had laid out a table with bread rolls, cheese chunks, biscuits, a churn of milk, and a black kettle bubbling on a primus stove. I stood, knowing I was hungry, but I had no money. Dad always said, "You get aught for naught."

One lady left her position, took my hand, and led me to the table. She offered me a tin cup of milk and biscuits. I sat on the wall opposite them as I ate. After I finished off what they gave me, the lady offered me a roll and cheese. Although the rolls were stale, they tasted good that morning, and for once I didn't care.

While I sat there eating, GranDad appeared with a battered brown suitcase in hand. He looked relieved at finding me and helped himself to a cup of tea and bread rolls. He led me back to the shelter and sat me on a bunk. We ate and drank in silence. Occasionally, he lifted his eyes to look at me and then stared back into his teacup.

He wasn't wearing his tie and stiff collar, unusual for him. His shirtsleeves were rolled up, revealing a bandage around his right arm. His head had a bandage too, and the right side of his face was swollen with heavy grazing and bloodstains covered in an ointment. He had changed his trousers, but I noticed he had a limp, and he sat with his right leg straight out. He reassured me that he had no broken bones and that he would be fine in a few days. Then he smiled and said, "If your mother could see you now."

I looked down at myself. My white cotton pajamas were covered in black dust, as were my feet and hands and, I assumed, my face.

"Better get you tidied up," he said. "I'm going to try to get you out of here today, to your mother. You have a bit of traveling to do."

Without further explanation, he took me by the hand and led me across the road into an empty house and through to the back scullery. He turned on the tap and gave a gasp of pleasure when the water came through. After washing his face and hands, he lifted me onto the draining board and he set about cleaning me up.

He stood me down on the scullery floor, reached into the battered suitcase, and handed me shorts, a shirt, a jumper, and shoes. "Sorry about the knickers" he said. "I couldn't find them." He helped me tie my shoelaces though I was able to tie them myself.

He eyed me approvingly and pulled a label from his pocket and attached it around my neck with a piece of string. "Keep this with you at all times," he instructed. "Your name is on it, as well as the address where you're going, where your mother is. I won't be able to come all the way with you. I'm needed here, so you're going to have to act responsibly and do as you're told until you get to your mother's. Got that, John?"

I nodded without really understanding. He couldn't explain more, and certainly he had no idea how the day's events would turn out.

He added, "I've made some inquiries and provided I can get you to the transport centre—if it's still there—someone will get you to a station, where you'll be put on a train to Epsom. The journey is half an hour or so. When you get there, your mother will meet you. If not your mother, someone will look out for you and take you to your new home. Have you got that?"

I nodded again.

He withdrew a ten-shilling note and two sixpences. "Now, if we're parted, use the money wisely for food. Just in case. It's not likely to happen." In those days, ten shillings was a fortune. Even at that age, I understood.

GranDad shook his head. "John, this is going to be a bloody war. Thousands have already been maimed, killed, or bombed out. You're better out of it."

Last night had been my first experience of being in a war, and death as yet had no real meaning for me. Even our hens and rabbits had "gone on holiday" as far as I knew. It took me longer to equate their empty cages in the backyard with the dinner I ate.

Taking me by the hand, GranDad led me through the house and outside. We walked up the road to our house, picking our way over roof tiles, bricks, and timber roof beams and crunching over broken glass, which we couldn't avoid.

GranDad's house windows had no glass. The door leaned against the porch. Past the stairs in the passageway, toward the back of the house, daylight filtered through. The kitchen and scullery extension to the rear had caved in. Much of the hallway ceiling was lying on the floor.

I wondered what Grandmother, who was house-proud, would say when she got home from work at the hospital. She stayed for days at a time, working long hours as a nurse. The first thing she did during her infrequent visits home was go from top to bottom, cleaning, disregarding the cleaning my mother had already done. Woe betide me if I didn't enter by the back door. She expected me to take off my shoes and put on slippers in the rear scullery before entering the rest of the house. I got away without doing it when Grandmother wasn't there, and so did GranDad.

Before she left with my younger sister, Mother worked as a relief in a hospital, and GranDad worked nights. We'd only been at GranDad's for six weeks, having moved from the other side of London, where Mother had problems coping with us and working after Dad had been conscripted into the army. We hadn't seen him since, and Mother never knew where he was although she did get the odd letter and read parts of it to us. His letter always started, "Sorry, I can't tell you much about where I am or what I'm doing except that I miss you all a great deal." Once he said he was living under canvas and looked forward to barracks and a warm, dry bed. Mother said that where he was and what he was doing was a secret. To me, and to all young lads, secret meant special. Dad was special.

Mother sat many evenings in the dim light of the blackout, reading Dad's letters, often with tears in her eyes. She missed him. We all did, but Mum wasn't the same without Dad around. She'd lost her sparkle and the laughter in her eyes and voice. She worried too much, especially about me and became overprotective. The once-relaxed atmosphere of home changed, and we were going through the motions of living.

GranDad left me in the hallway while he climbed the stairs to the bedrooms, warning me not to move until he said so. I heard him rumbling around upstairs, cursing. I wondered how Grandmother would feel when she returned and saw the desolation of the house.

At the family gathering Christmas last, after everyone finished dinner and started to talk and play games, the conversation turned to the First World War. Although I'd prompted GranDad to talk about the war, he hardly ever would. I'd seen his medals for bravery. "Four years of one muddy trench to another," he'd say. "Best forgotten."

"Tell you this," he said at Christmas, looking at the younger women, including my mother. "I hope you treat your menfolk better than I was treated when I got home." Most of my uncles were away on active service, and there was never any talk of the menfolk not returning. After further prompting, GranDad said, "Just dropped us off at the station. Straight out of the trenches. Through Germany, Belgium, and France by train. Boat across the Channel to Dover. Train into London. No bed, no stop, just travel. Slept and grabbed what food we could as we went along. Same kit bag, uniform, and rifle we came out of the trenches with. Nowhere to wash. Been promoted four times," he said, tapping the top of his left arm. "Three stripes and a crown but still couldn't get a lift home. Walked all the way, five or six miles. Still, many stopped me and shook my hand. Made it feel worthwhile. Suppose I could've waited for regular transport and a proper discharge. Sod them! I'd had a belly full of the army. Just wanted to get home as quick as I could. Anyhow, as I walked down our road, it felt good. I knocked on the door."

"Very loud," Grandmother interrupted.

"Grandmother opened the door, looked at me, and said, 'My god, is it really you, John?'"

"Stood there with a silly grin on his face," Grandmother added. "He looked different from the fellow who'd left me four years earlier. Much older, much thinner."

"But just as handsome," GranDad said.

"Yes! Well!"

"Did I get a kiss or cuddle?" GranDad asked. "No!" He pointed at Grandmother. "She told me to put my rifle and kit bag down in the hallway, took me by the hand, and led me through the house, out through the kitchen and scullery into the backyard. She ordered me to strip off—even my long johns—handed me a bar of carbolic soap and a scrubbing brush, and stood three feet away, spraying a cold-water hosepipe over me, commanding me to scrub here or scrub there."

"You were covered in lice," Grandmother said. "Couldn't have you in the house like that."

"Yes, but there is a limit," GranDad said. "Naked out there in the yard. When I told her I was cold, she made me pile up my clothes and set fire to them."

"I gave you a blanket," Grandmother said.

"Well, it wasn't the homecoming I expected," he said. "But you made up for it afterward." He winked at her.

She blushed, got up, and headed into the kitchen, saying, "I'm sure everyone would like a cup of tea."

GranDad sat in his favorite chair with a devilish grin, sipping his medicinal whiskey, as he called it. He puffed on his pipe and directed a smoke ring at me.

A chunk of plaster ceiling crashed to the floor, awakening me from my Christmas daydream. GranDad, who was still moving around upstairs, shifting furniture and cursing, came to the top of the stairs and called down to ask if I was all right. He nodded when he saw where I was and went back into the bedroom. Minutes later, he emerged with a large brown suitcase and a smaller one.

Downstairs, he handed me the smaller suitcase. "Here, try this for weight. Do you think you can carry it?"

I assured him I could.

"Good boy," he said, and added, "I've put in spare socks, underclothing, a jumper, and a shirt. That's all I could find in the mess up there. It'll have to do until you get to your mother. Put the suitcase down and come upstairs with me. I want to show you something."

Carefully we climbed the stairs and looked out the rear of the house through the bathroom door. The rear wall had collapsed. "See over there?" Granddad pointed to the houses, or what was left of them, opposite us. One was a rubble pile, and the dividing walls between the adjacent terraced houses had collapsed into it. Part of the remaining roof leaned dangerously into void. The house to the left was almost as bad with few walls intact, and the house to the right still had an upstairs floor, although it was cantilevered and resting on a rubble pile. The furniture had slid into the void. GranDad said, "The people in the house opposite were killed."

I took in the information without emotion.

"The house on the left was empty. The family are away. But the family in the house of the right had a baby. They didn't go to the shelters. They took refuge under the stairs. They're in a bad way with shock, but they got out alive. Notice the stairs," he said and pointed. "They're hardly affected. So the lesson is, if you get caught and can't make the air-raid shelters, park yourself under the stairs. Got that?"

I assured him I did. His explanation was graphic, not a lesson I'd easily forgot.

"Another point," said GranDad, "if there is a cellar, don't go in it. The house could collapse into it, and you could be buried alive. Take your chances under the stairs."

I nodded, and we descended the stairs, picked up our suitcases, and left the house. We turned right and walked up the road, picking our way through the debris. We walked for half an hour, passing bombed-out houses and factories, many still smoldering. The reek of burnt wood, flamed tar, and sulphur hung in the air. Pockets of firemen reeled in hoses and shored up walls as a temporary safety measure. Streets were awash with water from their hoses.

GranDad hardly spoke except to say it wasn't much farther. Judging by his face, I knew he was in pain.

At one point, a pile of rubble, where two or three houses had once stood, blocked the road. Bedding, bedroom furniture, clothing, and a baby's cot stuck out of the pile. We picked our way around. I stopped and froze. A hand and arm with a jacket sleeve stuck up out of the pile.

GranDad started pulling bricks away. I helped him. Two men in blue uniforms and tin helmets with red rings, indicating they were firemen, came out of one house. One shouted to GranDad, "It's all right, mate. There's nothing you can do for anyone there. We'll be going through that later."

After my grandfather and the firemen exchanged words, he took my hand and we continued on our journey. We passed piles of what I instinctively knew to be body bags, some folded over to make them small. Each had a label attached. Someone had left flowers. One row of bodies had tablecloths covering their top halves. I shuddered. GranDad told me not to look, but it was difficult to avert my eyes. The scene was so startling. I could tell four were ladies, two were men, and five were children.

Eventually, we came to a wide road that led into a square. The buildings had escaped the bombing. Army lorries filled the square. GranDad made enquiries and found a lorry going to the station. "Be there in a couple of hours with a bit of luck," he said, full of confidence.

He picked me up, gave me a hug, and put me on the rear of the lorry. After he handed me my suitcase, he said, "I'm afraid I can't go any farther. As I said, I'm needed here, but I'll catch up with you as soon as I can. Just do as you're told, and you'll soon be with your mother. There will be people along the route to help. If you have problems, ask and listen carefully to what you're told."

He helped other children and mothers with babies climb onto the lorry. Soon the lorry pulled away. GranDad stood, waving. He tried to smile, but his face looked grim.

Mostly I sat in silence as families talked to each other. The lorry stopped, and after the driver had a conversation with an air-raid warden, he detoured off the main road. We saw pockets of bombed outhouses, gutted factories, and warehouses. People stood outside their houses, guarding the furniture and belongings they had managed to salvage. Since the war, a code of behavior had developed that I eventually took part in: if someone left it and you needed it, you used it. The name of the game was survival.

We passed scruffy-looking men driving horses and carts, piled high with furniture. I'd seen them earlier when walking with GranDad, and he told me they were known as totters or rag-and-bone men. They bought furniture in one area and sold it in another because people were always moving around. Or they might have been moving the families and their belongings. There was such chaos it was impossible to know what was going on. I noticed there were few men of GranDad's age around.

At midday, we reached the railway station. As I got off the lorry, a policeman read the label around my neck and told me to go inside the station, through an archway, and wait on platform 9. I asked him to repeat what he said, but a lady with a baby said, "It's all right, Officer, I'm going the same way." She waved me to follow her.

We joined a crowd of mostly mothers and children. Some stood, but most sat on suitcases or upturned fruit-packing boxes. We sat for an hour or more. Except for a station porter who reassured people that the train wouldn't be long, we had no more information.

I didn't see anybody serving food, and except for people waiting for the train, the station looked deserted. The lady with the baby had hardly spoken to me, but when she opened a case and produced sandwiches, she offered me one. I thanked her and asked if I could get a drink. Another lady pointed to a tap on the outside wall of the public conveniences. After I drank, the lady with the baby smiled and asked if I felt better. I told her I did. She asked me about my family. When I told her about my mother and grandfather, my stomach felt nervous.

Everybody on the platform was unusually quiet. Even the babies only let out slight whimpers. I wasn't the only one feeling anxious.

The lady who gave me the sandwiches did something I found strange. She undid her woolen cardigan and her blouse, pulled them off her shoulder, took out a breast, and put it into the baby's mouth. I watched in amazement, embarrassed, for I'd never seen a baby fed naturally before. As I looked around, I saw other ladies doing the same thing. Feeling uncomfortable, I got up and walked the platform's length. When I returned, I saw that someone had laid out a trestle table with a tea urn, a tray of biscuits, and thick bread slices with corned beef or Spam. I joined the queue and, when it came my turn, offered my sixpences, but the server refused payment. The tea didn't have sugar in it, but the biscuits were sweet.

Suddenly, an air-raid siren sounded a long blast. Uniformed men wearing tin hats appeared from nowhere and ordered us down the stairs to the right-hand side of the platform into the underground corridors that formed part of the labyrinth of communication between platforms.

Nobody panicked or ran. Everyone went quietly down the stairs without any fuss or noise. Portable camp beds with grey and khaki blankets that looked distinctly unhealthy and probably harboured more life forms than they were meant to lined the underground corridors on one side. The corridor was dimly lit with oil lamps.

Two ladies wearing blue boilersuits and tin helmets sent people to the beds. They operated from a small hut built of sandbags with a corrugated tin roof. They were attentive to the mothers who had babies but ignored me. I supposed they had priorities but understood that GranDad's lessons about looking after myself had started. I put my suitcase on a bed and sat with my legs dangling over the side, watching the ladies to-ing and fro-ing. They produced bottles of warm milk and cartons of sandwiches, but I didn't get one.

I waited for about fifteen minutes before I went to the hut and asked for a carton. When a lady asked me how many, I said, "Two." I went back to my bed, undid my suitcase, and put the cartons inside. I felt satisfied because I was already learning how to survive and knew I had food for the next twenty-four hours.

After half an hour, people settled down and talked softly in small groups. Somebody started to hum. Singing broke out. I remember the first song, "Abide with Me." Other songs followed before a uniformed man appeared and told us that the air-raid siren was probably a false alarm and we could go back to the platform.

When we got there, a steam engine coupled to a dozen carriages hissed. A guard shouted out the numbers of the carriages and the destinations. I asked him which carriage I should be in. He checked the label GranDad tied around my neck and said, "Epsom for you, my young lad. Carriage three."

The train went along slowly, passing through the suburbs and into the countryside. I spent most of the time gazing out the window. As we stopped at various stations, I noticed platforms filled with soldiers carrying kit bags and rifles.

When we got to our destination, a guard walked up and down the corridor outside the carriage, shouting the station name. The lady with the baby told me to follow her. The platform was crowded with rucksacks, kit bags, and army men carrying rifles slung over their shoulders. Someone shouted, "Gangway, gangway!" and the soldiers cleared a path for the people getting off the train.

Someone grabbed me from behind and tossed me up in the air. My suitcase clattered to the ground. When I turned around, I came face-to-face with my father.

"Jesus!" he said. "Have we been worried about you!" He hugged me, and I hugged him. He picked up my suitcase and led me by the hand through the crowd into the waiting room, where he found a seat and lifted me onto his lap. His face creased in a smile, and his blue eyes sparkled.

It was the first time I'd seen him in uniform. I asked him what the stripe on his arm was for, and with a grin he said, "Staying alive and not being found out." He then explained, "My leave is over. Your mother and I waited for you most of the afternoon. She had to go an hour ago. She's waiting at home. I arranged a lift for you."

He gave me another hug and stood me down between his knees. "Now listen, lad," he said. "I'm off. I don't know for how long. I'll keep in touch with your mother. But in the meantime, you be a good boy and look after your mother for me."

How he thought I could look after my mother, I didn't know, but I felt a sense of responsibility. I promised I'd be good and look after her. He ruffled my hair and said he knew I would. I thought I saw a glint of moisture in his eyes.

"Here." He pulled out coins from his pocket.

I showed him the ten-shilling note GranDad gave me.

"Good lord," Dad said. "You must be something special. GranDad never gave me anything like that." He chuckled. "Listen, I've got to go shortly. I'll just make sure you get transport home. Your mother's worried about you." He took off his cap badge and pinned it to my jumper as he said, "Here's something for you."

Later, I found out that boys wore those badges with pride, a sort of comradeship.

He led me through the waiting room and out of the station and stopped a uniformed man who held a note board.

"Ah," said the man with a smile. "This is the young fellow we've been waiting for, is it?" He turned to me. "Okay, youngster, we know exactly where you're going." To my father, he said, "Don't worry, sir. We'll get him there. I'm sure his mother is going to be relieved." He led us to a lorry, opened the cabin door, and said, "There, my lad. You get up with the driver. I'm sure you'll enjoy that."

Dad gave me another hug and reminded me to be good. He walked away but gave me a wave before disappearing into the crowd inside the station. I didn't know it then, but it would be a long time before I saw the two people who'd waved good-bye that day.

It was early evening when we finally pulled away from the station, driving through to the town and up a hill leading out of town. The lorry turned off at points, dropping people off at the rear. I was the last one. We continued up the hill and out to an estate of about two hundred houses nestled on a common. Turning down a hill and round a bend, the lorry pulled up outside my new home. The driver jumped out and opened the cab door to help me down.

As I turned, Mother was there with open arms and a smile. She picked me up and gave me a welcoming hug. I was home—wherever that was—with a feeling of almighty relief at being reunited with Mother. That feeling only lasted for a while.

Chapter 2

LODGER IN THE BATH

Bombs on the Common

The events of the last twenty-four hours had taken their toll. I was worn out. Mother questioned me over a supper of leftover bread, soaked in hot milk and sprinkled with sugar and margarine. The meal revived me.

She wanted details, the full story. "How badly injured is GranDad? His head, arm, leg? Tell me more. What did GranDad say about his injuries? Did he give you messages for me? The house? What was the damage? Can he live in it? What's he going to do? Grandmother. How is she? You sure GranDad had no news of her?"

I had to go over the events several times, assuring her that GranDad didn't appear to be seriously injured. Obviously, he couldn't live in the house, but I didn't know where he was going to live or what he was going to do. I had no idea where Grandmother was or how she was.

Mother repeated her questions until she was sure I had no other information to give. Finally, she let me go to bed. I changed into pyjamas in front of the fire. My sister was asleep in the rear upstairs bedroom. Mother was in the front one, and I was to have the other small downstairs bedroom. It was the first time I'd slept in a bedroom of my own. Mother tucked me up in bed with a stone hot-water bottle and kissed me good night. The room was plainly furnished with curtains, blackout paper on the windows to keep the German planes from spotting me, and a bedside chair. A chest held Dandy and Beano annuals and other books. The bathroom meant no more pots, or poes, under the bed and no more telling-offs for wetting the carpet.

I lay in bed, thinking about the day, but the traumas weren't over yet. Something in the bed moved, and it wasn't me. I lay perfectly still, almost rigid. Something touched my thigh and then my arm. Instinctively I brushed my arm, threw back the bedclothes, and got up. I grabbed the chair and stumbled across the room. Standing on the chair, I found and flicked the light switch. In the middle of the bed, I saw a black spider the size of a tea plate. It was five inches across with long thin hairy legs and a bulbous body.

I froze to the spot, staring at the spider. It stared back at me. At first, I felt afraid, then revulsion, and finally anger. "Stuff you, mate! I've been through enough!" Somehow, that spider represented what I'd recently grown to hate. It became a German invading my territory, the personification of Hitler. I'd seen a caricature in the newspaper of a spider with Hitler's head and spider legs spread out all over the world.

He wasn't going to get me without a fight. I jumped off the chair, grabbed a book from the chest, and with all my might, swatted the spider. I leapt on the bed and pounded up and down on the book.

The bedroom door flew open. My mother marched into the room. "What's the commotion about?" she demanded.

Fearing a slapped bottom, I told her about the spider. "Should have seen the size of it," I gasped, my eyes wide-open.

She took a step backward into the passageway and told me to check if it was dead. I hopped off the bed and flipped the book over. "Yes," I said. "Flat as a pancake."

She disappeared into the kitchen and came back with a tea towel and instructed me to put the spider down the lavatory. I plucked it up with my fingers—all fear having left me—and carried it to the bathroom.

Mother backed up to allow me passage and called, "Mind you, flush it down the toilet." Even after I pulled the chain twice, she made me pull it a third time.

The episode wasn't quite over. An equally huge spider had taken up residence in the bathtub. Mother said she'd tried to get it with a broom but couldn't. I bombed it with a carbolic soap bar. Clunk! Splat! The soap hit the metal bath. We had a spider sandwich.

"Got it?" Mom put her head around the bathroom door. She took a pace or two back as I flushed the soap-entombed spider.

"Good for you, John," Mother said. "That's the way to treat lodgers who don't pay rent."

Mother was putting me back to bed when we heard a knock at the front door, and the voice on the other side boomed, "Don't open the door with the hallway light on." Mother told the voice to go to hell. After an exchange of words, it turned out that the local air-raid warden who lived two houses down the road had noticed a chink of light coming through the blackout curtains in my bedroom. He'd come to advise her, as his job required. She apologized and promised to sort out the problem in the morning. She told me not to switch on my bedroom light again. I figured I'd have to take my chances if I found more spiders. After this final episode, she tucked me in bed with another kiss.

In the morning, I found a front-sloping garden comprised of a rockery and lawn. Behind the house was a sizable garden, mainly lawn, with a path leading down to a wooden shed. A sunflower border grew on the left while climbing and rambling roses decorated the right. To the rear, separated by a dilapidated split-chestnut fence, was a row of allotments. Mother told me they had grown up almost overnight. Waste ground everywhere was being turned into vegetable gardens. She said that those with the energy, time, or inclination were allotted an area to cultivate free of charge. Mother had enough to do, she said, because she was going back to nursing.

Behind the allotments, a thick bamboo hedge screened an apple-and-pear orchard and a large greenhouse that was part of a country estate.

Mother was over the moon with her new home, especially the bathroom. It was a luxury to have hot running water heated by a back boiler fitted to the dining room fire. No more nightly visits to the backyard toilet. No more Friday night bathing in a tin tub in front of the fire.

Pride of place in the kitchen was a gas-fired washing machine fitted with a mangle, two rollers to wring out the wet clothes. A spring-loaded wheel on top of the mangle adjusted roller pressure, and the rollers turned by cranking a side handle. Flushed with excitement, Mother demonstrated the washing machine features. She had already used it twice in the two days she'd been there.

A letter from GranDad arrived the following week. Mother sat on the chair by my bed, holding the letter. Her eyes were red, and her face was wet with tears. She wiped her face on a hand towel and sobbed out, "GranDad's all right, but your grandmother was killed the night you were bombed out." She buried her face in the towel.

I worried about my crying mother and dreaded what might happen next. I could think of nothing to say, so I patted her arm while she cried. I felt dead inside. My emotions had been swallowed whole, leaving a chasm between thoughts, emotions, and soul, something that wasn't going to heal for many years to come.

After she stopped crying, Mother read me the letter. The hospital where Grandmother worked was hit directly. Twenty-eight patients and staff were killed, another forty injured. It wasn't possible to have a proper funeral, "a decent burial," as GranDad put it. There was no body to bury, no church service. He didn't even have her wedding ring or a lock of hair to save and treasure. She was part of the embers, dust, and shattered masonry. He attended a memorial service at the site of what had once been the hospital wing.

"GranDad's hurting," Mother said. "And there's nothing I can do for him. He says it's too dangerous to go and see him. He says he'll manage. He'll get by."

He had suffered a fracture to a leg bone on the night of the bombing and was now in plaster, hobbling around on crutches.

Mum smiled when she read what he'd written at the end of the letter: "It's the first time I ever worshipped a pile of rubble. It must be something to do with Stonehenge and my ancestry." Typical GranDad. He still retained his humour and spirit.

Mother grieved deeply after this, but she showed it more in her silence and mood than anything she said.

The next weeks passed slowly. I kept busy by helping Mother around the house, playing with my sister, and experimenting with woodworking tools I found in the garden shed. Wet days hampered my playing outside.

Mother said she must find out about school for me, but mostly—between meals, washing, shopping, and housecleaning—she sat in the dining room, writing to my father or looking into space. She'd take out my father's old letters and read them over and over with tears in her eyes.

It was an anxious time. No news arrived as to Father's whereabouts. I was instinctively quiet and amused myself. I played with an inverted clotheshorse on which Mother had thrown a sheet. It kept me and my sister occupied for hours. We transformed it into a camp, a playhouse, and setting for tea parties. We also played silhouettes, making shapes with our hands in front of a torch and took turns guessing what it was. Sometimes Mother played, but her heart wasn't in it.

She cheered up when three letters from Dad arrived on the same day. She read parts to me. Dad was concerned about how she was coping, whether his pay was getting through to her, and if she had sorted out my schooling. He didn't include news of where he was. He wrote that he found life tough and missed us all very much. Wherever he was, he was under a canvas and looking forward to getting into barracks. In the third letter, he said he'd been promoted to corporal, so extra money should be on the way.

Mother had told me she was worried about money. Because she had a passbook, she could go to the post office every week and draw some cash. "Not that it's much," she said. "I should have a larger allowance. The problem is paperwork, but never mind, we'll get by."

Her real worry was rent money for the house because she rented the house privately and Father hadn't left much money. She should have received extra entitlement to pay the rent because Dad was on active service, but the extra allowance hadn't come through. Application procedures were complicated and unclear. Mother had visited the post office but still hadn't received the appropriate application forms. She called the rent-collecting man, "the only person in the world who doesn't know there is a war on."

Mother usually took things in her stride and was rarely upset. She met situations head-on, said her piece, and let matters settle.

I was in the rear dining room when the rent man called. After Mother argued with him, she slammed the door and came back into the room, obviously flustered. "Idiot of a man," she said. "He knows the situation. I've told him three times he'll get his rent. He's got to be patient like the rest of us. People like him make my blood boil. I wish your Dad were here. No way would the rent man be so rude, the jumped-up weasel!"

I wished I were older. I'd sort out the rent man for Mum.

We heard another knock. I looked at Mother and she looked at me. "It's him again," she said. "Ignore him. He'll go away."

But the banging grew more intense. Loud banging, short pause, loud banging again. This carried on for several minutes.

"You'd better answer the door," Mother said. "I don't think I could face him at this moment. I might do him harm. Tell him to come back next week and shut the door on him if he argues."

Mum was right. He was a weasel of a man, although rat face might have been a better description, with his sallow complexion and dark hair matted down with hair oil. He wasn't very old, probably only a few years older than Dad, although at least nine inches shorter. He wore an ill-fitting baggy suit.

"Ah, the man of the house, I see," he said. "Tell your mother she has one week to find the rent, or she is out."

"I will pass that on," I said.

"And another thing," he added, putting his foot inside the threshold, "I need to make an inspection of any defects. I think I'll do that now."

"Sorry," I said. "Not today. Mother is upset. Come back tomorrow."

"Now," he demanded, moving forward and pushing the door open wider.

Anger boiled up in me. Where I got the strength, I don't know, but I grabbed the door and pushed hard with both hands. It rebounded off his foot, trapped in the threshold. When I pushed again, his foot had gone. Breathing heavily, I leant against the closed door with my back to his cursing on the other side.

I heard another voice. It was Chalky, as he was known—Mr. White to me—the air-raid warden who'd knocked on the door my first night in the new house. Chalky had become my mother's friend, bringing fresh vegetables and stopping for tea. He had called the morning after the blackout episode and helped Mother repair the blackout curtain. Chalky, who was in his late fifties, wore his First World War ribbons on his uniform with pride. His bearing and stature gave the impression he wasn't a man to be trifled with. He had the same honest directness on his face as my grandfather.

A knock startled me. "It's all right. It's me, Mr. White," he called even though I recognized his voice.

Mother came into the passageway. She'd heard what happened. "Don't worry," she said. "I'll open the door."

Chalky stood over the rent man, who was lying on his back with his left foot clutched in his hands. "It's broken," he moaned. "It's broken."

Chalky leaned over and felt the rent man's foot. "Doubt it," he said. "Just a sprain. What did you do, fall off the step?"

Before the rent man could explain, I said, "No. I shut the door on his foot. He tried to push his way inside."

"I see," Chalky said. "Perhaps someone could explain after I've sorted out this chap's foot."

My mother asked them both inside. She and Chalky helped the rent man into the living room. Chalky put a cold, wet towel around his foot and then bandaged it tightly.

Over a cup of tea, Chalky asked, "Now what is this all about?"

"Quite simple," Mother said. "He wants the rent, and my allowance hasn't come through yet. When it does, I'll pay him. I've shown him a form I have, explaining my entitlement to an extra allowance."

"Thought as much," Chalky said. "Had to have words with you about your manners a few weeks ago," he told the rent man. "This time you got your comeuppance. Much deserved from what I've heard around the neighborhood. Anyhow, how much rent is owed?" he asked.

The sum was twenty-eight shillings. Chalky unbuttoned his blue boilersuit, took out his wallet, and gave the rent man two pounds. "This should keep things going for a while," he said. "Don't worry." He turned to Mother. "Pay me when your allowance comes through." Chalky said he'd get the forms for mother to sign so that the rent man could be paid directly, a facility available if a husband was on active duty. "I'll get it sorted in a few days," he said. "Should be no problem." To the rent man, he said, "I don't want to see you around here again. If there are problems, come and see me. This lady has enough on her plate."

The rent man nodded, relieved as Mother that he didn't have to come back again. Chalky helped him hobble out.

After they'd gone, Mother smiled. "You're growing up fast. This will make Dad laugh when I write him. Now that it's sorted out, I can tell him about the problem. I'm sure he'll want to hear. Although I do wonder how he's doing now," she said wistfully.

In return for vegetables Chalky gave us from his allotment, Mother did washing for him. I liked him and he liked me. He said I reminded him of his son, who was missing after the evacuation from the Dunkirk beaches a few months earlier. His wife had died from heart trouble two years before. He had two grandchildren he hadn't seen for months. He hoped to see them when things quieted down. His daughter-in-law and grandchildren lived by the sea at Brighton. "Transport is the problem," Chalky said. "Not easy to move around at the moment."

I helped Chalky in his allotment at the rear of our garden. I'd help him lift and grade potatoes and carrots. He liked his carrots bunched according to size: big ones for stew, small ones for the dinner plate. Peas and runner beans were almost gone. He left some to dry for seed for next year's crop. Onions had flowered and were dying back.

I helped him plant winter cabbage and brussels sprouts. He planted carefully, using a line for equal spacing. We prepared the planting area with an old cast-iron garden roller. "The firmer the ground, the firmer the brussels," he said. Digging the runner bean pit took time. Chalky dug down three feet. It was like digging the foundation for a house. We threw old newspapers into the trench bottom to hold moisture, then added six inches of soil, a layer of horse manure and another layer of soil until we filled the trench. I collected horse droppings from the coal men and the greengrocers' carthorses. Scraps from the allotment either went on the compost heap or into the rabbit cages. Chalky showed me how to kill, skin, and gut a rabbit. At first, I was squeamish but soon got the hang of it. I so enjoyed the rabbit pie Mother made, and so did Chalky.

Down the road, a man kept pigs. Chalky bartered with him for rabbits and vegetables, so Mother had a pork leg to cook. The leg just fit into the oven and lasted for days. Leftovers ended up in a casserole or stew. We wasted nothing. Meat, like most things, was on ration and in short supply. Even coal was rationed.

My clothes were hand-me-downs. I didn't have any new clothes until after the war was over. Secondhand, repaired shoes and boots were all I knew. Chalky was good at mending boots by using conveyor belting.

Chalky told me he was making a surprise for his grandchildren. One day, as a special treat, he unlocked one of his sheds and allowed me inside. Boy, what a surprise! Surrounded by a woodwork bench, tools, a lathe and pots, paintbrushes, and wood pieces was a wooden rocking horse. He'd painted it a light grey with dark grey dappling. It had a real horsehair mane and a leather saddle with brass stirrups. It took my breath away. His grandchildren were in for a huge surprise.

Chalky told me how he made the horse. He fashioned the rocking gear from old perambulator bits, the saddle from a leather coat, and the mane from snipping the tradesmen's horses' tails. "With the horses' permission, of course," he said with a wink. I wondered if the tradesmen knew. The rocking horse's eyes were warm amber. "Had a bit of luck there," he said. "Found a teddy bear thrown on a dump. Not much left but the head with those pleading eyes staring out at me, amidst the garbage. So the horse has to be called Ted. What do you think?"

I agreed. In the next few weeks, I spent many a happy hour riding that horse as Chalky looked on, beaming.

Chalky took me out into the fields with him and taught me how to snare rabbits and throw a net to catch pheasants found in well-hidden openings in the woods where Chalky scattered corn. As we walked through the hedgerows and fields, Chalky asked me to name flowers, plants, trees, or birds that flew by. I became quite good.

In season, I picked wild rose hips for Mother. She made rose hip syrup, full of vitamin C to keep colds away. Her syrup tasted better than the alternative, cod-liver oil. I picked wild blackberries and crab apples, not only for pies but also for blackberry and crab apple wine. Chalky was partial to both. Dandelion wine was another of Chalky's favorites.

One day, Chalky took me fishing. Mother wasn't keen about it and warned him that I couldn't swim, but I went. When I caught a fish, I got so excited I fell off the bank into the river. I dog-paddled back to the bank, and Chalky fished me out. I was full of myself, being able to swim, when I got home; but Mother wasn't happy, so my fishing days were severely limited. From that day on, Mother went with us.

While working the allotment or walking across the fields, I was always aware of planes droning overhead. Chalky pointed out the planes and named them for me. Our main fighter planes were the Spitfires and Hurricanes. The main bombers were the Lancaster and Halifax. The common German planes were the Messerschmitt twin-engine fighter-bombers and the faster single-engine fighters, the Messerschmitt 109s. We also saw formations of Junkers, JU 87s, Stuka dive-bombers, the Junkers 88 fighters, and the larger Heinkel and Dormer bombers. Before the daylight bombing stopped due to heavy German losses, we saw squadrons of German planes and escorts silhouetted in the sky, all heading for London.

Many afternoons or early evenings, I watched dogfights overhead with one or more planes spiraling to the ground in a billow of smoke. Chalky and I had a lucky escape one afternoon. A Heinkel bomber broke up in midair. The fuselage crashed to the ground two hundred yards from us. One minute the plane was flying high above the ack-ack flack, and the next it disintegrated. In those early days, I seldom heard an air-raid siren. The distance guns gave a late warning.

Occasionally, I'd see pilots or crewmen dropping slowly to earth in parachutes. More often than not, the crew went down with their planes. The drone of the planes and the radio news bulletins that Chalky or Mother listened to in the evenings were a constant reminder that there was a war on. It was difficult not to be aware of the enormity of the effort and sacrifices being made. The Battle of Britain was on, and I was living through it.

Chalky came around one day, pushing his large-framed bicycle, a sturdy machine with a three-speed hub operated by a lever on the crossbar and separate front and rear brakes. He had fitted a saddle and two footrests on the crossbar. He asked Mother if he could take me for a ride. She eyed the seat with suspicion, but when Chalky set me on the crossbar and made adjustments to the front rests, she let me go off with him.

"You might like to come out on night watch with me," Chalky said to me. "History is being made. You should see some of it so that, God willing, you can tell your grandchildren."

We went up and down the hill outside our house, each time coming down the hill faster. Around the bend to the hilltop on the final run, Chalky leaned the bicycle, letting out whoops of glee. I hung on tight, enjoying the thrill of speed and confident in Chalky handling the bicycle. Mother was at the gate on our last descent. I waved at her.

"Chalky, you are a raving lunatic," she said after our last run.

He grinned. "Just fun. But safe, I assure you."

"Really! At your age," she said.

"Don't feel old," Chalky said.

"You men never grow up," scoffed Mother. "All the same, looked dangerous to me."

"Not a bit of it," he said. "Much safer than the bike I rode in my youth."

"They are made better now," she agreed.

"Not much different," Chalky said. "It's the ride that was different."

"How different?" Mother asked. "Riding off cliffs?"

"No. I rode to the trenches in the First World War on a bicycle. Call that dangerous."

"Go on with you." Mother laughed.

Chalky changed the subject. "Can I take this young man with me tonight on fire watch? I assure you, I'll be careful."

"Suppose it will do him no harm," she said. "But he'll have to nap for a couple of hours this afternoon."

"See you at seven, young lad," he said.

"Come at six," Mother said. "I've got rabbit pie on the go. It's going to be chilly tonight. You could do with a good meal."

When Chalky arrived that evening, he put bottles of his blackberry and crab apple wines on the table along with a box of vegetables. After we ate, he patted his stomach. "My, that was a meal fit for a king," he said. "I shall not be hungry tonight." He turned to me. "Come on, John, let's get going."

Mother wrapped me up with a coat, scarf, and balaclava to keep my head and neck warm. We took off up the hill, past the row of shops at the estate's edge, and along the road, headed across the bridge over the railway line to the top of the hill and across the main road. Twice Chalky stopped and pulled off the road to let lorries go by. "They can't see you in the dusk," he said. "Those blackout deflectors on their headlights cause hundred of road deaths. I think it would be safe to have good lights and stop when there's an air-raid warning. Damned stupid," he muttered.

We traveled a mile down a wide grass track with common and woods on either side. Finally, we climbed a hill to a massive building. It was the grandstand of Epsom racecourse, the home of the derby. We were up on Epsom downs.

We climbed the outside stairs to the grandstand's roof. There was a battery of searchlights and two ack-ack guns surrounded by walls of stacked sandbags.

Chalky exchanged words with the men and introduced me. One man brought me a tin hat and told me to keep it on at all times as he adjusted the strap. He also gave me cotton wool for my ears. "If we get busy and I forget," he said. "Although it's supposed to be a quiet night."

Chalky showed me a small hut made of three deep sandbags and open back and front with a shallow blast wall outside each entrance. The roof was corrugated iron sheeting stacked with sandbags. "Won't keep out bombs," he said, "but keeps out the draught and bullets. Not that we have any cause to worry so far. Been quiet for several days now. We're here for four hours until the night shift." He looked up and added, "It's a clear night. It's possible we could see some action. You never know. Anyhow, have a look at this gun."

He put me in the gunner's seat. Everything was larger than I expected. Chalky explained how the turntable worked and how to raise and lower the gun turret. "Bit old-fashioned," he said. "The more modern ones are faster. Still, it's better than nothing."

I suddenly realized Chalky was a gunner. He hadn't said anything.

He showed me the searchlights and introduced me to the crews. Afterward, I sat in the makeshift air-raid shelter where a paraffin primus stove heated a water urn. Periodically, the men came in and warmed themselves with a cup of tea or cocoa. They offered me cocoa, a type of hot chocolate made without milk and sugar, but I didn't like it. The searchlights played in the sky, crisscrossing each other and working in patterns.

After spotting a plane, an observer with binoculars shouted, "Okay, one of ours" or "Hold it steady, not sure" or "Right, one of ours." At ten o'clock, a siren went off, so close it startled me.

A man grabbed a telephone hanging on the wall and rotated a handle on the side. He listened and then replied, "What's up?" He replaced the telephone on the hook and hurried outside, shouting, "Bombers coming in! Due south. Could be this way in five minutes."

The searchlights turned toward the south. Across the downs and into the distance, searchlight after searchlight came to life. I heard ack-ack firing above the wailing of air-raid sirens. Lights flickered across the sky. I saw the silhouettes of barrage balloons.

An observer shouted, "There! Over there! Eleven o'clock!"

I looked out of the rear entrance over the low blast wall. In the silhouette of the searchlights, I saw the outline of planes.

Someone shouted, "There must be over one hundred heading for London!"

To me, they looked to be flying along quite slowly. I heard men shouting that if the planes kept coming, the gunners might set a shot at them.

Chalky appeared in the other doorway and told me to sit on the floor below the sandbags. "Safe here as at home," he said. "Possibly safer. They'll avoid us once we open up. Only a direct bomb hit can affect us." He lifted my balaclava and stuffed the cotton wool plugs into my ears. "Be firing in a few minutes, with a bit of luck," he said and left to return to his gun.

Minutes later, all hell broke loose. All around us, gunfire sounded. After ten minutes, firing ceased. Chalky and other men came back. He pulled the cotton wool from his ears, so I did too. "Flying too high," he said. One man came on the phone and passed the message, giving an estimate of the direction and height of the flight path. He said there were one hundred to one hundred fifty planes.

More men joined us, most with grim faces. "London's going to get a pasting tonight, and there's little we can do about it. Never mind. We did our best."

I could still hear ack-ack fire in the distance.

"Maybe they'll have better luck farther toward London. They won't bomb from that height. Still, stay on alert for their return. Unlikely though. They usually use a different route out."

After a mug of tea, Chalky took me outside. Toward the northeast, we saw an orange glow on the horizon, which gradually grew brighter and brighter. "That, my boy," he said, "is London burning. God knows how many they've killed tonight."

I wondered about GranDad and what he was doing.

The next half hour passed quietly. Occasionally, someone made a comment. We heard air-raid sirens in the distance. The phone rang. The man who answered repeated the message, "Some are coming back this way. The flack must have been too heavy for them. They're unloading their bombs on the way out."

We heard explosions in the distance. Gradually they came nearer. Chalky estimated the last one was five miles away. "Time for action," he said and left after telling me to put the cotton wool plugs back in my ears. Nothing happened for half an hour. Chalky came back. "Too far over to the east for us to get a crack at them. Never mind. There'll be another night." He shook his head. "And I thought it was going to be quiet tonight."

When the night relief shift showed up, Chalky said it was time to go. After he exchanged greetings and information with the new shift, he led me down the stairway and pedaled me home. He had little to say, lost in his own thoughts, I imagined.

As we approached the turning into the estate, we saw lights ahead. The rows of houses across the green had been in complete darkness when we passed by. Chalky exclaimed, "There must be something wrong. No one would have lights on like that if there wasn't." He pedaled faster. As we turned into the shopping precinct at the top of the estate, the problem became clear. The shops' windows, the upstairs windows, and the large plate glass display windows had shattered. Glass covered the pavement and the adjacent service road. A dozen people stood outside the shops, some boarding up windows, others sweeping glass.

A bomb had dropped a hundred and fifty yards away, just on the edge of the common. There had been no warning. Fortunately, no one was injured. About thirty other houses along the opposite road lost their windows too. People were annoyed that the estate had no air-raid warning siren. Chalky told them there were plans to install one soon. He went to the phone box near the post office and the general stores—the only phone on the estate. There were no private phones, but Chalky had a special communication set at home.

When Chalky got off the phone, he reported that a German bomber had been hit by antiaircraft flack and crash-landed about five miles way near Chessington. The plane wasn't able to gain altitude or reach its target, so it discharged its bomb load before trying to land. There was a trail of reported bombings for five miles. The estate hadn't been a deliberate target. It had been an isolated case. Chalky said Epsom received three bombs, and deaths had been reported.

With that grim news, the shopkeepers stopped moaning about the lack of warning. Chalky and I helped them clean up. He made several trips to the phone, checking on air raids, worried about the light showing.

When we got home, Mother was agitated. When a bomb dropped on the other side of the estate, the house shook.

Chalky said it was a stray bomber, discharging its load. "Nothing out here to bomb," he said. "Nevertheless, the sooner we get an air-raid siren fitted up on the estate, the better. One can never tell. Also, I'm told those that want them can have air-raid shelters put up in their gardens. Like most shelters, they're only good for blasts. Nothing will save one from a direct hit."

"Enough excitement for one night," Mother said. "Off to bed with you, young lad."

The next morning, I woke up thinking about air-raid shelters. I told Mother what GranDad said about parking under the stairs. Mother thought it was a good idea and set about cleaning the jumble under the stairs and making up temporary bedding. "Just in case," she said. "May have been a stray bomb or two. Be glad when they get their sirens fitted up. Had enough of surprises."

Over the next two weeks, people erected Anderson shelters in their rear gardens. To build one, you dug a pit three feet deep and six feet long by six feet wide. Block or shuttered concrete lined the pit on a concrete flow slab. The walls and roof were made of heavy-gauge corrugated iron. Hessian sackcloth covered the small front entrance to keep out the draft. You shoveled the excavated earth back over the corrugated iron and placed a mound of earth four feet high a few feet from the doorway to act as a blast wall.

There must have been a financial contribution to be made for having an Anderson shelter installed, which explained why we made do with sleeping under the stairs.

Our neighbor, an elderly man who lived on his own, had an Anderson shelter put up in his rear garden. His grown-up daughters visited occasionally, but we hardly noticed he was there. After the construction, he told my mother we were welcome to use the shelter. Mother thanked him and said she would but hoped there wouldn't be reason.

At last, we got an air-raid siren on the estate. It was tested the first week at ten in the morning. The first night a bomb dropped nearby, just behind houses on the estate's edge, the siren didn't go off. Chalky said there was no report of aircraft in the area that night, so it must have been another stray bomb.

"Too near for my liking," Mother said. "We're sleeping in the shelter tonight." She made arrangements with the neighbor who said he wouldn't be coming down.

We stayed up to nine o'clock. Mother led my sister and me out with a torch around to the shelter. She prepared beds earlier in the day, happy to try things out. It was cozy inside with two bunk beds either side of the entrance, two a foot above floor level, and two just above ground level. Mother put me at one end of a top bunk and my sister at the other end. She said it would be warmer that way. She slid onto the other top bunk and sat up in bed, reading by her torch. My sister and I went off the sleep.

I was the first to awake in the morning. It took me a few seconds to remember where I was. When I heard heavy rain outside, I reached over and pushed the Hessian curtain aside to look out. It was teeming with rain. Judging by the light, it was early. As I turned, I felt water and looked down. Water stood a few inches below my bunk's base. I hopped out of bed, stood in the doorway, and pushed the Hessian curtain aside. Then I reached to shake my mother's shoulder. When she woke, I pointed and shouted, "Water, water!"

Mother told me to come in out of the rain and look after my sister. She assured us she wouldn't be long and returned minutes later with coats and Wellingtons. She sent us home and followed later with the bedding. That was the first and last time we tried an Anderson shelter. "Could have drowned," Mother said. "I nearly put you in the lower bunk."

I wondered if I would have drowned or if the water would have awakened me.

We stayed under the stairs on siren nights for a few weeks until a thick-sheeted metal table called a Morrison shelter was delivered. The table had a bed underneath. Mother and my sister slept under the table, but I preferred to sleep under the stairs.

Chapter 3

DAYS OF DARKNESS

The British Isles got hammered from the Luftwaffe. Talk continued all around me of the devastating bombing raids by the German bombers. Every major port and city in the British Isles came under attack and suffered brutally. It was impossible not to be aware of the situation. Constant reminders came from the radio, from Mother and her friends who exchanged information while they waited in food queues, and our mine of information, Chalky.

Through the autumn of 1940 to midsummer 1941, the figure of British losses and casualties were shattering and compounded our sense of helplessness in combating the nightly attacks. We heard how well our services—fire, ambulance, and hospitals—coped. The number of enemy aircraft shot down was likely exaggerated. Who was to know? When Winston Churchill came on the radio, which was frequently, he gave a stirring speech. I liked to listen to him. Schoolboys recited his "Hour of Darkness" speech:

We shall not flag or fail.
We shall go on to the end.
We shall fight in France.
We shall fight on the seas and oceans.
We shall fight with growing confidence and growing strength in the air.
We shall defend our island whatever the cost may be.
We shall fight on the beaches.
We shall fight on the landing grounds.
We shall fight in the fields and in the streets.
We shall fight in the hills.
We shall never surrender.

We placed a great deal of faith in Churchill. Chalky was a fan. He said, "We stand alone against the most sophisticated and lethal war machines the world has ever known," a possible extraction from one of Churchill's speeches. He added, "I'll tell you this, young John. We've been here before. They didn't lick us then, and they won't this time. Not without a hell of a fight anyhow." This hard-nosed attitude wasn't just Chalky's. It was part of any talk around, crystallized by Churchill's speeches.

Mother was more down-to-earth. "The situation as I see it is this," she said one day in a rare talk about the war. "The British Isles are getting a pasting, and there's little we can do about it. Our fighter pilots in the Battle of Britain last summer stopped the daylight raids, but it only meant the Luftwaffe switched to nighttime bombing for which we don't have much defense. No doubt we'll come up with something," she added. Ever optimistic was Mum.

The next day, I told Chalky what Mum said, hoping for a more confident viewpoint. "It will change," he said. "It has to. Come into my study, and I'll try to explain." Chalky was quite perceptive, short-term anyhow.

I liked Chalky's study. It was full of treasures, wood carvings he'd done; mementoes from the First World War—German bayonets, helmets, cap badges, pictures of him in uniform—a globe; stamp and cigarette collections; books on butterflies, trees, plants, and fish; and geographic magazines with pictures of the world's countries, their geography, people, flora, and fauna. I spent many happy hours in Chalky's study.

Chalky had a dartboard in the middle of one wall. A picture of King George VI hung to one side, a picture of Winston Churchill on the other, with a picture of Hitler stuck on the dartboard.

He showed me Europe and the British Isles on the globe. I was surprised at how small the British Isles were relative to the size the British Empire once was. He also showed me countries I'd seen in the geographic magazines and countries where his stamps came from.

Chalky opened a drawer and pulled out a large European map. He pointed out Germany and the countries overrun by the Germans. He pinpointed Dunkirk where his son was last seen alive. He reached and tapped a wooden bookend and smiled. "Just for luck, can't give up hope yet." He explained the politics of how Germany had risen from the First World War. Most of it went over my head. "Trust," Chalky said. "Trust. We should never have trusted him," he said, meaning Hitler.

"You see," Chalky said as he unfolded another map and showed me Russia's outline. "Hitler is right up against Russia's southern border. This is the key." He stabbed Russia with his index finger. "Tons of oil and other resources. Hitler needs oil to sustain his war effort. The longer we hold out, the better our situation gets. There's no oil here. We're just a thorn in Hitler's side.

"Our salvation depends on which way Hitler jumps. Or what Russia does. Can't see Russia staying out of this mess much longer. They're under too much of a threat. But on which side and how long? Politics is a dubious subject. Surely the Russians know by now not to trust Hitler. So far, he hasn't kept one single word he's spoken, certainly not in the political arena. I suspect he must be getting his oil supplies from Russia. Can't see where else. He must have used up his stockpiles. He must be paying for oil, but it's not his style to pay for what he believes he can take.

"I don't like Joe Stalin or his politics any more than Hitler, but at the moment, we're not in a position to pick our friends. Let's hope Stalin and Hitler fall out. It could be our salvation. It would give us the much-needed time to prepare ourselves better."

Chalky turned to the globe. "Oil is here and here," he said, stabbing at Russia and the Middle East. "If Russia proves difficult, and it will if Hitler threatens, he's going to have to go for the Middle East's oil. He'll have to fight on three fronts: Britain, the Western Front, and the Middle East. With us, the English Channel is his problem. We have a lot of fighting men here, and our fighter planes are superior around our shores. To get his men and tanks across the channel, get a foothold and subdue us is going to cost Hitler dearly. That's why he hasn't come over. His armies have been standing in the French cliffs, looking at us for nearly a year now. I think he'll try to contain us and go for Russia. That's what these continued bombing raids are about. He could have come if he wanted to. He's not prepared to take the risk. Let's hope he continues to think that way. It would be a bloodbath for sure, and I for one wouldn't like to predict the outcome."

I understood only some of what Chalky told me, but the essence of what he said stayed with me all my life. On reflection, I recognize his observations were very perceptive.

"There's another aspect for more hope," he told me. "Do you want to hear it?"

I nodded.

He showed me America on the map. "Got some good friends out there from the First World War, and we still keep in touch by letter. A very powerful country," Chalky said. "Got a population over twice ours. More than rival us in sea and airpower. They're helping us out at the moment, but it's a drop in the ocean to what we need. They're going to have to come into the war sooner or later. Look." He dotted his finger around the globe: Canada, Australia, New Zealand, India, and other small countries were rat-tatted out. "They're all in it with us," he continued. "The distance is not important. This is a world war that could decide the outcome of the direction of the free world for several generations to come. Who knows where Hitler will stop if he takes us over? Can't see him leaving the Americans alone. They wouldn't be his only threat to world dominance. No! He won't stop with us. Not that he's going to find it an easy task, you can bet on that. The Americans are going to wake up one day to the threat. The sooner the better. Boy! What a difference that would make! Just imagine Hitler taking on us, the Russians, and the Americans. He wouldn't stand a chance. It could happen. Let's hope it does. It's certainly a possibility."

The sound of "Germany calling, Germany calling" broke into radio programmes. In a BBC announcer's voice, Lord Haw-Haw—later hanged as a traitor—gave exaggerated figures on the latest bombing, the port or city, casualties, deaths, and other demoralizing news he dug up. He started his broadcasts with "Our glorious" this or that, have done this or that, and ended with a comment that the British Isles should throw in the towel. Mother stuck two fingers up at the radio. Nobody believed what Lord Haw-Haw broadcast, but it kept our own newscasters busy, putting the facts straight and giving out more news than the government probably liked.

Cities had devastating losses, lives, and casualties in the thousands most clear nights. It became normal to try to sleep through the wailing of air-raid sirens and ack-ack battery fire and to see men in uniform with guns slung over their shoulders walking around the estate or in town on our occasional visits there.

Life around the estate went on as best it could, but the atmosphere was grim. News of the war, bombings, and husbands, sons, and daughters away was the general conversation topic.

For a treat, Mum took us to the pictures or a concert by a military band in the marketplace. Just to get out and do something was a relief for her, although a visit to town meant a three-mile walk, as there were no buses or any other forms of transport, not for civilians anyhow.

Racehorses still trained on the Epsom Downs. Occasionally, I went with Chalky to watch them gallop, usually when he had to attend for training or day duty. One day midweek, there was a race meeting, including a funfair. I got a label to tie on my jacket so I could ride free on everything. Chalky shot at traveling ducks with an air rifle at a fairground stand. At first, he missed, and that hurt his pride. He complained to the fairground worker that the sights on the rifle were out. But he finally got the hang of it. When I returned, he'd won two rag dolls, a set of flying ducks, and a vase.

"Nice shooting," the worker said to Chalky.

"Nice profit," Chalky muttered, pleased with his performance. He gave me a rag doll to take home to my sister and the vase for my mother. "Know anyone who wants a set of flying ducks?" he asked with a laugh.

Finally, I was going back to school. Across the other side of the estate nestled in the far corner of the older houses was a small chapel. It was really a large tin shed, but nonetheless, inside was an altar, fine drapes, stained glass windows, and a table with hymnals and prayer books near the entrance. Pews lined either side of a central aisle leading to the altar on which stood a brass crucifix. Handmade hassocks with needlepoint Bible scenes lined the pews. A tin hut it may have been, but it had a spiritual feel.

Two ladies set up a school at the chapel for three hours each morning, and Mother made arrangements for me to attend. She found a quick route skirting our road, and by negotiating a plank over a ditch, we followed a path that led up to the chapel. After a few days, Mother let me go on my own.

School was fun. Children between the ages of five and twelve attended, twenty-five in all. We sat on the hassocks and used the pews as tables. Mornings started with a prayer for our king and queen, our fathers and mothers, our soldiers and sailors, and our airmen and merchant seamen. Then we sang two or three songs. One lady belted out the tunes on an old upright piano, wedged between the front pew and the altar. I picked up the tunes and words to the songs—good old chestnuts, still some of my favorites: "All Things Bright and Beautiful," "Onward Christian Soldiers," "Morning Has Broken." When the rain resounding off the tin roof tried to drown out our singing, we'd let it rip, egged on by the other teacher and an older girl who conducted us with gusto from the front of the chapel. Occasionally, we said a special prayer for an individual, usually one of the children's father, who was missing or injured on active service. The school had a personal and family feel to it.

The older children helped the younger ones with their alphabets, sums, and writing. I delighted Mum and Chalky by writing a page on my new life, including Chalky as part of my family. I'd had a flying start with the exercises Mum and Chalky had already given me. School brought it all together. Within three weeks, I read picture comics and recited the lower order of my multiplication tables. I looked forward to going to school as much as I did my trips into the countryside with Chalky.

The few shops to the top end of the estate were rarely open. Notices outside gave a day and time when rations would be on sale. We'd been issued ration cards with coupons for an ounce of cheese, meat, butter, flour, sugar, and other items. Mother always managed to find a meal. I was never aware of going hungry. We ate what she put on the table at mealtimes, no questions. We either ate or went without. My favorites were stews and dumplings. Quaker oats for breakfast was the norm. We always had milk. Even at school, they gave a cup of milk midmorning.

Most remarkable were the preparations for a German invasion. In a drive for raw materials, iron railings disappeared off front garden walls. Aluminum pots and pans, used for recycling into planes, were stacked high in front of the shops. Road signs disappeared. Huge, deep, open dykes, acting as tank traps, opened up near many crossroads. Concrete pillbox gun emplacements were built at major road intersections. Work started on cleaning woods and common land to make way, as it turned out, for potatoes, corn, sugar beets, and other root crops.

We saw wires running across bridges, which were obviously being mined. Areas of land approaching major intersections had signs warning of mined areas, but they must have been bluffs because in later years, the signs came down as quickly as they went up.

Everywhere we traveled, which wasn't far, we saw teams of servicemen putting up defenses. They may not have been fighting, but they were getting ready. Preparations were probably happening all over the country. Somebody was expecting an invasion.

News came in mid-May that changed my life, for a while at least. My sister and I were going away to a safer place. Mother couldn't come with us because she was required to go into nursing and to billet other nurses. She told us a relief medical centre was going to be set up nearby.

We heard radio reports about the events that caused the surprise announcement from Mother. Liverpool had been bombed seven nights in succession. There were over 3,500 casualties, more than half fatalities. Then we got news that over 500 bombers hit London in one night. The preliminary estimate for casualties or deaths was as high as 4,000. More bombing raids were expected. Those "high up" decided the raids, and those to come were a final softening-up exercise prior to an invasion. In fact, it was Hitler's final fling before turning to Russia.

Orders went out that every able-bodied man and woman—this included my mother—in designated areas were to be voluntarily mobilized, along with property. Officials advised that children within certain age groups be evacuated to safer areas. Mum said it was a directive. There was no option. The massive defense undertaking had been in the planning stages and was finally being put into operation.

Chalky came around and said he had a directive to give up two of his bedrooms. "But with luck, I'll get two male nurses," he said.

Mum gave him a look that made him go red. She said, "We have more than enough to worry about without you chasing a couple of nurses around the house."

"Wonder where they'll hit first," Chalky said.

The invasion was becoming a fact, at least in most people's minds.

Both my sister and I had to have a medical exam prior to evacuation. The morning came all too soon. Mother woke me early and told me to have a bath. An old gentleman who lived a few doors down the road had cut my hair the day before. It was a lovely style. He'd put a pudding basin over my head and clipped the exposed hair. Then he tapered it into the freshly exposed skin. I looked like a shorn sheep at springtime. When Mother saw it, she couldn't hide a grin, and Chalky said I'd get by the sergeant major with that haircut. Anyhow, I was shaved, shorn, and bathed. Mother gave me clothes I hadn't seen before and a hurried breakfast. Soon after, we were on our way.

The medical and disbursement centre was in a large school hall on the other side of town. It took an hour and a half to get there. Mother took the pushchair even though my sister, coming on five, didn't need it. She used the pram for carrying shopping back from town, a weekly trek I dreaded. As we set out across the common, I called out plant and tree names as we passed. After ten minutes, Mother said I was getting on her nerves, so we walked the rest of the way in silence.

There were over a hundred children with mothers in the school hall. After documentation, we had to follow signs marked Boys and Girls. My sister and mother headed down the left corridor, and I joined the file of boys headed down the right corridor. I had to carry a white card and wore a number around my neck.

Every ten yards was a table with doctors and nurses dressed in white coats. At each station, a nurse took my card to write examination notes. At the first desk, a nurse scrutinized my hair with a fine comb, probably looking for fleas or ringworm. I think she had trouble finding my hair—what little there was—let alone ringworm. Next, a nurse examined my teeth, then my eyes. I stood against a wall, placed the white card over each eye, and read the letters on the opposite wall.

At the next table, I had to strip to the waist. A lady doctor checked my back and chest with a stethoscope. When she asked me to drop my pants, I nearly died of embarrassment. She poked around my privates and then had me turn around and bend over while she pulled my cheeks aside. While I was exposed, ladies and girls and the general public walked by. I wondered how many of those nurses would have like their privates poked in full view. This was my first experience of public nudity but not my last.

After a nurse inspected my ears and throat, I had one final stop. I rolled my sleeve up for a dab of wet cotton and an injection with a huge needle they used over and over. They directed me back into the hall where I waited for Mother. She took my card to a desk and spoke with a doctor about my examination.

He reported that I was fine but needed three teeth out. Unfortunately, a makeshift dentistry was on the premises. With little wait time, I sat in the dentist's chair with a gas mask over my face. I came around, minus three teeth, which they placed in a cardboard box for me to take home. I swilled foul-tasting water and went back out to Mother. I'd had enough of that place. My sister came away scot-free.

"There," Mother said. "All over. Just some things to collect, and we can go home." She disappeared into an office while we waited outside. When she came out, she had a bundle of paperwork and two small canvas square boxes with shoulder straps, which she gave my sister and me to wear. "I'll explain when we get home," she said.

The boxes contained red rubber gas masks that attached to the face with straps. Each mask had round clear glass eyepieces and a round filter system that hung under the chin. They were claustrophobic. I thought I looked like Mickey Mouse with it on. Luckily, I never had to wear it, but I received lectures on the need to carry it. It was another of the Germans' dirty tricks that we anticipated.

Mother had a long talk with my sister and me before we left for the train station. Chalky came around to wish us good-bye and good luck. "Not going for long, I hope," he said. "I shall miss you."

I wore a dark raincoat, two sizes too big, turned up at the cuffs over my short trousers and jumper, and a cap that had seen better days. I had GranDad's battered brown suitcase. Across one shoulder, I carried the gas mask; and over the other, a brown herringbone, striped tin containing sandwiches for the journey. Around my neck hung a string with a large buff ticket with my name and address printed on it with a ringed bold number.

An official directed us to our carriages—boys and girls rode separately—but he didn't know exactly where we were billeted and who would look after us. "Don't worry, madam," he said. "We've shipped out thousands. As far as I know, we haven't lost one yet. The train is scheduled to leave at nine o'clock. They'll be there in three to four hours." That wasn't accurate, but it wasn't his fault. How many similar journeys were to be like that one, I didn't know. It was a journey I would only want to do once.

Once I was settled in a carriage, Mother put my case in the rack above my head. Other boys ranging in ages up to about twelve sat in the compartment. One little lad could only have been about four years old, a little younger than my sister. He was with his older brother.

Mother hugged and kissed me and gave instructions about being good, and then she went off with my sister farther down the train.

As the steam engine pulled the carriages slowly out of the station, I caught sight of Mother and other women on the station platform, waving and crying. Mother had watery eyes. I wasn't sure she saw me even though I had a seat by the window.

We all sat quietly for a while, occupied with our own thoughts. The pit of my stomach felt raw with nerves. I was afraid of what lay ahead and felt no sense of excitement or anticipation. When I saw Wales on the map, it appeared far away. I felt I was being thrown into a chasm while being told, "Don't worry. You'll land safely." Our evacuation was an act of faith all around, and my faith was wearing thin. I was full of doubts. Where was I going? Would I come back? Who would look after me? Would I see my mum and dad again? I'd been given assurances, but nothing tangible to hang on to. I needed a bit of Chalky's optimism. I thought about the events and places I'd been the past few months: Chalky's study, the allotment, the night in the Anderson shelter, GranDad's house.

Suddenly, I was jolted out of my daydream by a bang as the railway compartment door opened. A man in a dark green boilersuit with a tin hat stood in the doorway. The white flash band on his arm with a red cross indicated he was a first aider. "Right, lads," he said. "Everyone all right?" When we nodded, he continued, "The toilets are at the end of this corridor." He pointed to the left. "Just around the corner is a milk churn and tin cups. Help yourself if you fancy a cup of milk. Be sure to return the cups. We're a bit short. You can wash the cups out in the toilet washbasin. If you feel crowded, there are one or two empty compartments farther along. Any questions?" There were no questions. "Oh yes," he added. "If you hear a Klaxon sound off a long blast, kneel down in the aisle, put your hands over your head [he demonstrated], then put your face down on the seat. It will be a precaution should there be any stray bombs about. We're not expecting any problems but might as well be prepared. Repeated short blasts on the Klaxon and we want you to put on your gas masks. Do you know how to do that?" We nodded. "Two long blasts means it is all clear. Should only be on the train three hours or so," he said, and with that, he shut the door and continued to the next compartment.

One boy took out his gas mask and stared at it before fitting it over his head. He adjusted the straps to the rear, wriggled his head around before taking if off and putting it back in its satchel. I took my gas mask and my sandwich tin off my shoulders and put them beside me.

Two of the older boys started a conversation, asking what school we went to, what our dads were doing, and what we've seen the week before. Incidents came up: a café in town had been bombed, causing a considerable loss of life, and the building where one boy's mother worked lost all its windows. The boys knew from my accent that I was from London and were intrigued by my story of the bombing. I said we moved to Epsom because it was safe.

"Not anymore," said an older boy. "Don't think anywhere is safe. Though I'm told they haven't had much trouble where we're going." When I asked where we were going, he said, "Not exactly sure. Somewhere in the Welsh countryside. We're not being sent to a town. My mother said we'd go to a disbursement centre and then on from there. Don't know our final destination. Still, be glad to get away from those 'moaning minnies' of air-raid sirens. Haven't slept in my own bed for six months. Been in the air-raid shelters most nights. School closed two months ago. Lost all its glass. Not that we spent much time in school. Always filing backward and forward to the air-raid shelters." He paused. "Shit. Just to get a good night's sleep. Mum says she closes one eye and then the next when she's walking. Gives her some rest. On autopilot, she calls it."

The question of a possible German invasion came up. The boys' parents expected it. The atmosphere in the compartment was gloomy. Nothing in our chatter dented that gloom.

I went to the toilet and then stood in the corridor, hanging on to the steadying bar and watching the passing countryside out the window. When I got back to the compartment, two of the boys were gone and so was my sandwich box. I made a fuss, asking the other boys if they'd seen it, but they hadn't. I didn't think they were genuine. They helped me look on the top shelves to see if someone hid it as a prank, but it wasn't there. Someone stole it. I sat in the corner of the compartment, bemoaning my luck.

One boy opened his box and offered me a sandwich, and I accepted. It tasted foul, peppery; but it was food, and I was hungry. I decided to get some milk, so I put my gas mask over my shoulder, stood on the seat, and got my suitcase down. I went along the corridor to the milk churn, armed with all my possessions, taking no more chances. As I passed the last compartment, which was empty, I noticed my lunch box inside on the seat.

The milk churn stood in the corner by the emergency door. It was half full. A copper ladle hung on the side. There were no cups, so I went back to the empty compartment, picked up the bottom half of my lunch box, and returned to the churn, where I filled it half full. I returned to the empty compartment and drank the milk from my lunch box. After finishing, I watched the countryside again. In the distance, I saw planes. One had smoke streaming from it as it descended rapidly. Before the plane passed out of sight, it started to spiral.

A loud Klaxon sounded. I didn't panic, but I moved quickly. I opened my gas mask case and put the mask on the seat beside me. Then I knelt, put my hands over my head, and buried my face in the seat. The Klaxon wailed.

The carriage jerked and shuddered and came to an abrupt halt. The brakes screeched and glass shattered. A minute passed before the compartment door flew open. "Stay there, son," a man's voice ordered. "Be back in a moment. Looks as though we've been hit."

The Klaxon stopped. General commotion from farther down the train was drowned out by the sound of two short bursts on the Klaxon. I jumped to my feet and looked out the window. The bank to the side of the train sloped gently up to wooden fencing and a hawthorn hedge. First aiders and women in nurses' uniforms ran alongside the embankment. Two nurses carried rolled-up stretchers. Another carried a first aid box.

I stood at the window, watching people pass by until a man opened the door and told me to get my possessions and file out of the train up onto the railway bank. Boys followed along behind him. I packed my gas mask, picked up my suitcase, and joined the line of boys filing out. However, before I reached the carriage end, I saw a large open tin nearly full of sandwiches. I popped into the compartment, emptied my gas mask out of its case and filled the case with sandwiches, fastened the flap down, and popped the mask inside my coat. I joined the boys on the railway embankment. A man with a megaphone ordered us to climb to the top and wait for further orders.

At the top, I saw a road on the other side of the hedge. When I turned around, I saw what happened to the train. The carriageway I'd been in had blown out glass in two compartments. Part of the roof of the next carriage was missing, and windows were blown out. In two other compartments doors hung off their hinges.

From the conversations around me, I realized enemy aircraft had attacked us. I watched as nurses rushed to the damaged compartments. A few boys emerged, their arms in makeshift slings. Others had bandages around their heads. Two boys had bandaged legs. First aiders carried them up the embankment. Others hobbled up the hill with assistance. Men and older boys farther along used a section of fencing to flatten a hedge, providing a walkway to the road.

Planes flew overhead. One or two came in low. I knew they were ours by the circular marking on the wings. A megaphone boomed out again, telling us to stay calm and stay where we were. Help was on the way.

We sat on the embankment in the sun for about twenty minutes until two army lorries pulled up. Two soldiers manned an antiaircraft gun mounted on one lorry. Shortly afterward, two ambulance lorries arrived.

The ambulance crews rushed to the damaged compartments. Two came back after a few minutes with boxes, both marked with first aid signs. The megaphone voice announced that the train would not be going on because a bridge farther down the line had been damaged. They would ferry us by lorry to pick up another train. We might have to wait for two or three hours.

I found a patch of grass, sat down, opened up my gas mask flap, and started on the sandwiches I'd found. They were fish paste, and I liked them. Ten minutes later, conversations around me stopped. When I looked up, I saw everyone staring at the damaged compartments. The ambulance crew carried four bags. Everyone knew what was inside. Even I knew. I wasn't hungry anymore. I felt sick. Some boys around me were visibly sick. Our planes circled around us, very high up.

I must have dozed off in the sun. A soldier woke me. "Come on, son, on your feet."

There were only about fifty of us left on the embankment. The steam train shunted the empty carriages slowly backward. Someone had boarded up the damaged windows.

I climbed up into an army lorry parked in the roadway. Once it was filled, we drove off through the country lanes for ten miles until we arrived at a country village station. I had no idea where it was. There was a tea urn, a churn of milk, and hard scones laid out for us in the waiting room. I wasn't hungry, but I did have a cup of milk and pocketed two scones.

The adults told us to be sure to go to the toilet before we boarded. I'd already gone twice in the embankment hedge but went again before we boarded a train with no corridor. We had an adult in the carriageway, a lovely lady who handed out comics and kept the conversation going. Soon she had us playing I Spy.

The train moved slowly. One by one we dozed off. The lady woke us and told us we were nearly there. The sun was low in the sky. We'd been traveling for twelve hours. The train pulled up at a small station whose sign read Talgarth. Twenty of us got out. The train had stopped at other stations while I'd been asleep.

A reception committee of five ladies and a gentleman met us on the platform. Our train lady spoke to them and left, waving as she departed. The reception committee said they expected us earlier in the afternoon and wondered what happened. The older boys explained. The committee assured us we were safe and going to be well looked after.

I saw a sign over the ticket office with the words Talgarth Welcomes You. It was also printed in another language: Welsh, of course. We'd arrived in Wales, minus seven boys, as it turned out. I wondered if my mother knew I was all right, and I wondered where my sister was.

Chapter 4

FINDING NEW FRIENDS

The reception committee escorted us in groups out of the station and down a narrow path leading to a riverside. We walked along the bank path, which led us into the village centre. In front of us stood a village hall, the disbursement centre.

Inside were tables laid with food and drinks: sandwiches, cakes, scones, blancmange, soft drinks, and tea. It looked like preparations for a party. They encouraged us to take a plate and help ourselves. I ate heartily and resisted the instinct to hide food in my pockets.

While we ate, two ladies armed with files took details off the buff card around my neck. They double-checked my parents' names, my address, and my sister's name. Everything tallied.

"Where is my sister?" I asked. When I'd asked earlier at the station, I was told not to worry, I'd find out soon.

One lady flicked a sheet over, ran her finger down a list, turned back to the first list to cross-check, and said, "She's at Hay with the other girls. We're only taking boys here. It's policy."

"What is Hay?" I asked.

"It's a town about eight miles away," she said. "Don't worry. I'm sure she's being well looked after. We'll arrange for you to see her in due course. In the meantime, we'll get you sorted out. That's the priority at the moment." They moved on to take details from other boys.

After we finished eating, they asked evacuees to line up on the far side of the hall. We were to meet the people with whom we were going to be billeted. A door opened, and people filed in with papers in their hands. No doubt the papers gave details about us, listing salient facts or problems our mothers might have mentioned.

The men and women walked up and down the line, smiled at us, and welcomed us to Talgarth. They said they hoped the journey hadn't been too tiring. In what I guessed was a sort of interview, one or two asked if I had brothers or sisters, how my mother was coping, and what my father was doing. Everything seemed pleasant.

A large bluff man and his wife stood opposite me. He had a red face, large ears, and bulbous staring eyes. He wore an old tweed jacket open at the front, a half-open shirt with no collar, and a pair of baggy, dirty brown corduroy trousers that fastened over his ample belly with a huge leather belt. His trouser leg bottoms were tied with string over muddy old leather boots. The couple stared at me for over a minute before fixing their gaze on someone farther up the line. The man pointed at me and spoke to his wife. The vibrations I got from them were not good.

She came up to me, peered in my face, and asked, "You in good health?"

"Yes," I said.

"Do you wet the bed?"

"Frequently," I said, instinct coming to my rescue. "It's been a problem." I lied.

She went back to her husband and spoke to him. When he scowled at me, I couldn't stop myself from putting my tongue out at him but quickly pretended to lick my lips. His scowl deepened before he turned away to pay attention to another boy. I sighed with relief.

Within seconds, a lady who had spoken to me earlier came up and said, "You're John?"

"Yes," I replied.

She said her name was Mrs. Davies—one of many in town I later discovered. "Would you like to stay with me?" she asked. She had a kind face, and I thought she was nice to ask, but I didn't really have much choice in the matter.

"Yes," I said, glancing down the line to see where the large bluff man was.

"Good, come with me." She took me to a table where another boy about my age stood. He had a bandage around his head. "I'll take these two," Mrs. Davies said to the lady behind the desk.

The other boy's name was Phillip. We nodded at each other and followed Mrs. Davies down to the far end of the hall to tables with hand-knitted jumpers, socks, scarves, Wellingtons, trousers, pyjamas, pants, and vests. Nothing looked new, but they were in good condition. Mrs. Davies helped us choose a set of clothing, including two pairs of shoes and a pair of Wellingtons. Loaded up, we followed her out of the hall and down the road to her house. After we told her we didn't want anything to eat, she had us washed and tucked up in our bedrooms. I fell asleep and didn't wake up until morning.

I found a change of clothes laid out for me on the end of the bed. Mrs. Davies came into the bedroom after hearing me move around and showed me where the bathroom was. She told me to wash and get dressed before joining her downstairs in the kitchen where she had breakfast for me.

She had a large family kitchen with a solid fuel range for cooking and hot water. There was a deep white porcelain sink with a wooden draining board, a Welsh dresser, and cupboards for pots, pans, and crockery. A clothes dryer rack that she could lower on pulleys hung adjacent to the range. Beyond the kitchen was the scullery for washing clothes. Leading off the kitchen was a walk-in pantry with shelves of bottled fruits, jams, sacks of potatoes, onions, carrots, and other root crops. On a hook at one end hung a side of pork.

A large pine table with six carved pine chairs stood at one side of the kitchen. Mrs. Davies had laid up a place for me. I had milk and cereal, followed by eggs and bacon—far too much—but I did my best to finish.

While I ate, Mrs. Davies bustled around the house, popping her head inside the door occasionally, giving me a smile, and then disappearing again. I sat on my own after I finished eating until she came back and sat at the table with me.

"I'm afraid you don't have a playmate," she said. "Not as yet anyway." When I screwed up my face in puzzlement, she said, "Phillip."

"Oh yes," I said, having forgotten about him.

"He was sick in the night. Had to get the doctor in. Appears he's suffering from a concussion caused by a nasty crack on the head he got during the journey. The doctor took him into the cottage hospital for a few days."

She asked me about my train journey, my home, and the bombing. When I told her about the events, she took my hands and gave them a squeeze. She said things were going to be better now, and she would write my mother. She promised to find out where my sister was and arrange for me to see her. Mrs. Davies was a fine lady. I'd been fortunate with my billeting.

Philip stayed in the hospital for several weeks. We went to see him at weekends. Besides his head wound—a nasty gash—he had damaged ribs.

His mother came down after three weeks with a baby and a two-year-old. She told us little about the bombing except that the situation was still very tense. Nobody quite knew what was going to happen, especially now that Germany had invaded Russia. After staying with Mrs. Davies for a further few weeks, she left with Phillip to live with her sister at Leominster in Hertfordshire, not far from the Welsh border.

The news that Germany had invaded Russia first came to me over the radio at breakfast. It was at the end of June. The news was abrupt: "In the early hours of this morning, Germany launched a major offensive against Russia." The radio announcer went on to give brief details. "The Germans opened up the offensive in a broad front from the Baltic to the Black Sea. Reports are coming in of intensive bombing raids carried out through the night and early hours of the morning over Russia by the Luftwaffe."

Mrs. Davies, who had been sitting at the table with me, appeared startled. After composing herself, she turned to me and said, "At least, we have an ally. We're not on our own anymore." I told her what Chalky said about Russia, and she nodded in agreement without comment. She rose to clean the breakfast table in silence, deep in her own thoughts.

Later, I asked Mrs. Davies if she had a map of Russia. She found a book of world maps. She went through the maps with me, showing me the Baltic and Black Seas and the borders of Russia and satellite countries. She said I could keep the book with me while I stayed with her. As news came through, Mrs. Davies pointed out the cities mentioned.

One day she came in with a globe she had borrowed and placed it on the Welsh dresser. What amazed me was Russia's size—something I hadn't picked up during my conversations with Chalky. By comparison, Germany seemed small, England even smaller.

News about Russia was grim. The Germans were sweeping through it. Because Germany had turned its attention to Russia, the intensity of the bombing back home has eased, and the threat of invasion receded.

The summer of 1941 passed peacefully for me. Mrs. Davies's old rambling house was on the roadside opposite the river Wye. To the front of her property was an unused café with a billiard table. This café became my playroom on wet days and my workroom at other times as Mrs. Davis insisted I keep up with my sums, reading, and writing. She got me to write an occasional page home to Mother and sent it off with a letter she wrote. She enjoyed reading books to me, and she liked listening to me read to her.

She had grown-up children who would arrive and stop over for a few days. Mr. Davis worked at a steelworks at Port Talbot, and their youngest son worked in one of the many Welsh coal mines. Like everybody else in the British Isles, they worked long hours and seldom came home.

A few days after arriving, Mrs. Davies took me down the road to the Williams farm and introduced me to a farmer, his wife, and their two sons. One boy was a year or two older than I was, and the other was four years older. I was welcome to come around but understood that if I was there, I had to help, not watch or get in the way. The older boy was known as Di; the younger lad was David. Di offered to show me around the farm, an invitation I gladly accepted. We walked out of the farmhouse and across the lane to the farmyard entrance. The drive was lined with trees—elms, ash, and imposing oaks. Intermingled with hawthorn, elderberry, and hazel was a variety of wildflowers.

A natural stone hedge enclosed the farmyard. The yard itself was a good size, probably an acre. A long low building on the left contained the milking parlor or shippen, as it was known. Inside the gate was the dairy, where workers brought in the milk from the shippen and prepared for sale and distribution. The buildings across the yard were a series of stables and hay and straw barns. Tudor-like in appearance and built of red brick, the barns were two stories high with oak piers and beams. Heavy oak trusses supported the dark red clay tile barn roofs.

Inside the stables were two enormous shire horses used for ploughing and other heavy farmwork. In the smaller stables, Mrs. Williams kept horses for delivering milk around the village. Eventually, I learned to handle the milk carts myself. The low building to the right of the yard contained pigs. In the small semienclosed area stood a wood-fired cast-iron urn. The urn was used for boiling up pigswill collected from the local hospital and school each day. Root crops and corn were mixed into the swill with water, brought to a boil, and ladled out for cooling in buckets before being fed to the pigs.

All the farm implements in the large barn were fashioned to be wheel-driven by horsepower, one shire horse. Controlling horse and machinery at the same time took remarkable skill. David, and Di in particular, were accomplished at it.

In one corner of the building was a large circular grit wheel used for sharpening ploughs, sheers, and other implements. An array of hand tools, including scythes, pitchforks, sledgehammers, posthole borers, and two-handled saws hung on one wall. The mixed smells of the farmyard was rather pungent at first, but after a few days, I didn't notice it.

Plump dark brown chickens and geese ran around the yard. Di said the geese kept the foxes away since foxes don't like geese. He gave me a pail of corn to scatter amongst the chickens and geese. As I scattered the corn, the chickens pecked furiously. Two geese came at me, hissing. Di shooed them off and told me not be frightened. "They'll get used to you," he said. "Besides, they're good watchdogs."

I admitted they frightened me until I grew used to them. They were like dogs in their instincts, becoming friendly quickly.

Through the yard, a five-barred wooden gate opened to a field of two or more acres dotted with apple trees. Thirty or forty sows—most in pig, Di said—occupied the field. The pigs had rings in their noses to stop them ploughing for roots and turning the field into a quagmire. Sows rummaged around in the grass, others sunned themselves, and some slept under the trees.

I arranged to help in the milk parlour over the weekend, just for an hour or two. Mrs. Davies woke me at dawn. I dressed in shorts, jumper, and Wellingtons. When I got to the farmyard gate, forty or more black cows stood around the parlour doorway. I found out later they were Frisians. They looked like huge black and white predators to me. I stared at them. They stared back at me. I stood on a gate run and shouted, "Help!" No one heard me above the mooing. I'd nearly given up when Di appeared.

He laughed and clambered over the gate to lift me down into the yard. "Don't be frightened," he said. "They're timid creatures, really. Look, I'll show you." He took my hand and led me into the herd, pushing them away with his hand as we went along. When we got to the other side, he said, "Now you do it. Go on. Walk through them." I hesitated. "Go on," he encouraged. "I'll be right behind you."

I started forward and pushed on a cow, but it didn't budge.

"Slap her," Di said. He leaned over my shoulder and gave the cow's hindquarter a slap, pushing her aside.

The next time I tried, it worked. I discovered that if I got to the front where the cows could see me and put my hand out to push them away, they moved themselves. I was full of confidence.

The cows literally queued up at one door to the milking parlour, entered for milking, and left by a door at the other end afterward. A bar operated by a rope and pulleys from within regulated the flow of cows.

Di took me into the parlour to watch the cows being milked. Four farmhands sat on stools by the side of the tethered cows, pulling and squeezing on the cows' teats. Squirts of milk flowed into buckets underneath.

"Hi!" shouted a voice from behind a cow. The weathered brown face of a man my grandfather's age grinned at me. "You must be John," he said. "Heard about you. Welcome to the parlour."

"Thank you," I said.

He turned the cow's teat around and pointed it at me, splashing a stream of blood-hot milk in my face. I stood there drenched. Peals of laughter ran out from Di and the man. Di gave me a towel and helped me mop up.

Still laughing, Di said, "I've been caught a few times myself. It's Owen's favorite trick. Dad gives him hell if he catches him doing it."

Owen came around, wiping his hands. "Sorry," he said. "I just couldn't resist. You're a full-fledged parlour man now."

Splat! The cow Owen had been milking relieved herself on the floor and up Owen's trousers. The smell made me choke, but Di and I couldn't stop our laughter. Owen muttered something in a strong Welsh dialect about bloody cows.

I became a willing worker and thoroughly enjoyed helping out. Owen and Di took me under their wings, showing me how to do the tasks properly and keeping an eye on me until they were confident I understood what I had to do.

Owen tried to teach me to milk, but my hands weren't strong enough, and I was wary of the cow's hind leg. If I did anything wrong, up came its leg, sending me flying across the milking parlour. The trick with a "stroppy cow," as Owen called it, was to put one's shoulder in between the hindquarter and the leg. This prevented the cow from kicking. When I tried, I couldn't reach the teats properly.

"Good try," Owen said, picking me up from the parlour floor for the third time. "For the time being, we'll try something else until you grow a little more."

However, I did master milking before I left the farm.

At first, my job was to operate the gate that let the cows in. Then I made a compressed form of feed. I put a shovelful of cake made of corn, molasses, and chopped swede into a mincing machine contraption that compressed the ingredients into squares. After that, I put the squares into the feeding trough as each cow came through.

I also helped in the birthing of calves, "calfing down," Owen called it. The two front feet came out first. Owen tied a rope to the feet, and as the cow heaved or contracted, he pulled gently on the rope. Gradually, the nose and head appeared. I'd pull on the rope, and Owen would put his hand inside the cow to ease out the calf's shoulders. Once the shoulders were out, the calf slipped out. Owen cut the umbilical cord, its lifeline to mother, he said, and tied it into a knot on the calf's stomach. He wiped off the mucous with straw and put the calf in front of the cow. She licked the calf clean. Within hours, the calf was up and, with help from Owen, sucked at its mother.

Sometimes there were problems—a stuck calf, retained afterbirth, a relapsed womb, the mother's innards needing to be put back—and that's when Owen's experience and knowledge came into play. He took all problems in stride. He even performed mouth-to-mouth resuscitation on a calf that wouldn't breathe at birth.

"Lost an odd calf," he said. "Never lost a cow yet. Better touch wood." Superstitious was Owen.

Watching and helping with the piglets' birth was less strenuous. They seemed to pop out one after the other, often more than a dozen. They were tiny things, all pink with their eyes closed as they sucked at their mother's teats. Owen kept watch on the piglets for the first few days. He encouraged them to nest in an oil-heated corner of the calving sty under a diagonal steel bar. This prevented their mother from lying on them.

I enjoyed helping bring in the cows from outlying fields and ladling out the milk to customers who brought in their own pint and quart pots. Milk from the pails went into a vat. It flowed from the vat through a honeycomb of small pipes that had cold water running over them. The cooled milk went straight into the churns to be sold. Mrs. Williams made butter or cheese from the cream that had been skimmed off into a smaller churn.

Mr. Williams spent most of his time in the fields or orchards. The orchards produced apples for cider making. At the right time, workers shook the trees, shoveled the fallen apples into piles, and collected them for the cider makers.

Getting in the hay, helping pile up the bales to weather, stacking them on the hay wagon, and unloading them at the barn was hard work. David and I worked together. Neither of us could manage a bale on our own, especially the heavy ones at the edge of the field that hadn't completely dried.

But the hardest task was harvesting the potatoes. They were lifted mechanically and left in rows to be collected and put into Hessian sacks. Small potatoes and damaged potatoes went into a sack for pig food. Large ones were sacked for distribution and sale. The whole village turned out at potato harvest time.

Mr. Williams would often give me money as payment for my efforts. He'd put his hand in his pocket, count out a few coins, and hand them to me. "Well earned," he'd say. I gave the money to Mrs. Davies, who kept it in a jam jar for me, as I didn't need money.

By the end of summer, I'd become an old hand on the farm. Even the geese ate corn from my hand. They followed me as I wandered around the yard and hedgerows at the field's edge, picking up eggs the chickens laid and putting them into a basket. I put aside the largest brown eggs for Mrs. Davies.

It wasn't all work and no play that summer. On wet days, David and his friends and I played in the hay barn. We built a camp high up in the haystack by hollowing out a few bales. We crisscrossed the spare bales over the top of the wall to provide a roof and created something like an igloo.

A rope hung over one of the roof trusses. We climbed up a ladder to the top of the stack and launched ourselves off, hanging on to the rope for dear life. The momentum of the arc projected us out through the barn doors fifteen feet up in the air over the farmyard and back onto the side of the stock so we could fall onto the loose hay. Swinging kept us occupied for hours.

We played another game by improvising with the belt conveyor used for loading the bales high on the stack. We moved the conveyor to create a slope to the top of the stack and placed a bale on it so that we could slide down the conveyor.

When he caught us at this game, Mr. Williams gave us a serious ticking off, not for the danger but for the number of bales we wrecked. He didn't spoil our fun completely though. After making us clean up the mess, he bound up a bale tightly with baling string and gave us a couple of loops. He repositioned the rope we had over a pulley so we could use the same bale by hoisting it back up to the top of the stack each time.

Other wet days, the boys and I played billiards or darts at Mrs. Davies's. She made us a nice tea with cakes and scones piled high with homemade jam.

On drier days, we roamed the fields and woods, helping ourselves to apples from any orchard we happened across. The elder boys made catapults from a hazel sapling fork, elasticized rubber they found, and a leather stone holder cut from a boot tongue. Some boys were good shots. We never got near enough to damage rabbits or birds, but we had great competitive fun aiming at tin cans placed in hedgerows. An older boy could hit a can three out of five times—not bad shooting.

On hot sunny days, we wandered down to the river, which, except for a narrow channel or flow, varied in depth from a few inches to eighteen inches. We waded up the river, jam jars in hand, lifting large pebbles and small rocks, beneath which we found catfish. They stayed almost motionless as we turned a stone or rock so we could catch them easily. With their large heads and wide mouths, their faces resembled a large cartoon cat. After an hour or two of filling up our jars with fish, we returned them to the water.

Just down the river from the stone bridge, the river flowed over flat rocks, creating a small rapid of three feet. In the deeper part, we had great fun floating from the bridge over the rapid, laid out on a blown-up inner tube from a lorry tyre.

Occasionally, Di took us to the other side of the village, up past the cottage hospital to a part of the river that had deep pools. We waded the river, fly-fishing for trout. They were good eating, cooked over a campfire on an improvised spit.

Every two weeks or so, I got a letter from Mother telling me how she was getting on. She worked long hours at a hospital, looking after soldiers and bombing victims transported out of London. She never went into details but gave the impression it was long, hard work with little time off. Mrs. Davies wrote back, enclosing a page or two from me, which would take me some time to finish as Mrs. Davies corrected my initial attempt and made me rewrite it.

Once Mother wrote to say she had two younger nurses billeted with her. She quite enjoyed their company. After reading her letters, I'd often sit and think of home. Although I was well looked after, it wasn't the same as home.

Occasionally—usually on a Sunday afternoon—Mrs. Davies arranged for me to be picked up and taken to visit my sister. Going to see her was a pleasure for several reasons. She was always glad to see me, and I was happy to feel a connection with home. Also, I enjoyed the welcoming reception because I was treated as a special visitor.

The journey to Hay took us out of Talgarth along country roads and through fields of cows, sheep, orchards, and corn. The countryside stretched up to the backdrop of the Black Mountains on one side and endless vistas of flowers, fields, woods, and rolling hills on the other.

Located just outside of town, the house where my sister stayed was an imposing stone-built terrace house with a large vegetable garden and spacious lawn, running down to a brook. My sister was billeted with two older sisters who got along with each other. They were early in their retirement and enjoyed having my sister and her new friends staying with them.

My sister had a large room on the top floor of the house. From the dormer windows, she had views over the countryside to greet her each morning. Her room had a matching flowery bedspread and curtain drapes. She had dolls and children's books lying around and a small desk. The older sisters had gone to a lot of trouble to make her comfortable and provide her with her own space.

There was an old chicken house in the garden that had been converted into a Wendy playhouse. We spent the afternoon playing tea parties in the house, paddling in the brook if the weather was fine, and playing rounder with my sister's guardians. Invariably, we took walks over the adjoining countryside, taking in the beauty of the place.

The tea was always a slap-up affair with more than I could eat, and I left with a box of cakes and biscuits and my favorite, a bag of homemade toffee. This would be topped up with a book or comic. I was always sorry when time came to leave and felt disappointed that the rules didn't allow boys and girls to be billeted together, not even a brother and sister.

One Sunday a commotion outside my bedroom window awakened me. About sixty men marched four abreast along the road, flanked by their leader. He was a tall man of upright military bearing, shouting commands, "Left, right! Left, right! Halt! Slope arms! Stand at ease!" The platoon marched up and down the road, turning around and passing backwards and forwards several times.

I dressed quickly and slid down the stairs to the front playroom and opened the window for a better view. Most of the men were in their forties or fifties, but there were younger men and one or two in their sixties.

Some wore military uniforms—army, navy, and air force—not modern ones but those of a bygone age. Others wore navy blue and dark green boilersuits. Farmworkers, obviously just come from milking or fieldwork, wore baggy corduroy trousers, shirts with no collars, leather, sleeveless waistcoats, and flat corduroy hats known as ratting hats. Some wore brown trilbies, and one had a pith helmet like I'd seen in pictures of our First World War Indian regiments.

Old issue 303s slung over some shoulders. Twelve bore shotguns, but others had air rifles and rifles fashioned from pieces of wood. The tall man flanking the parade wore a full-army military uniform complete with brass buttons, a flat guard's hat with a chinstrap, and straps on the arms of his uniform. He had rows of campaign ribbons over his breast pocket. The slant of his cap peak partially hid his face, but his large grey moustache was in full view. Every inch a soldier, he marched with his arm crooked, nestling a black ebony stick with a large brass head under his armpit.

I saw Owen in the parade, shotgun sloped over his right shoulder and his favourite large-bowled pipe clenched firmly between his teeth. Others—shopkeepers and tradesmen—I'd seen around the village, and there were also farmers who did business with Mr. Williams.

By now, Mrs. Davies joined me. We watched in amazement and bewilderment. As the parade moved off toward the village centre, I heard chugging noises coming nearer. Three old tractors, two Nuffields, and a third that must have come out of the ark with cast-iron wheels running on steel rims headed for the village centre. Each had been painted in blotchy dark grey, dark green, and brown camouflage paint and had a fence post strapped over the bonnet with rope. The posts projected over the bonnet fronts by about three feet. On either side were raised flags, the Union Jack on one side and the red Welsh flag sporting a gold dragon on the other. It looked like a carnival was about to begin. In a way it was.

Mrs. Davies gave me an explanation. "That, my dear," she said with mirth, "is our home guard. It's made up of men who are either too old or unfit for frontline service or in reserve occupations vital to the war effort. Many are First World War veterans. Others have seen some service. They meet twice a week, or least they disappear for a couple of evenings. They're on maneuvers this morning. It happens every six weeks."

"What about the tractors?" I asked.

"I think they're supposed to be tanks," she said, and her face creased with a smile. "It's reported that arms and tanks are located at military depots the other side of Brecon. In the event of an emergency, they'd whisk the arms over here. At the moment, priorities for arms are with our regular troops. The home guard must make do for the present and just stay ready and alert. I think arms would be here quick enough if needed. Some of the men go off weekends for tank-and-arms training. Others spend time up at an old quarry some three miles away, practicing firearms and grenade drills. I must admit they all seem keen to play their part in defending the town, should it ever come to that. They have all sorts of plans worked out. The exercise this morning is defending the village against an attack.

"The enemy are the home guard from Brecon," she continued. "They are possibly somewhere out in the hills at the moment. It's all taken very seriously. There's a bigger turnout than for a local rugby match, and you can't get much more serious than that. There's a lot of pride at stake. It should be fun today."

I ate my breakfast in a hurry, but Mrs. Davies delayed my departure by reminding me I hadn't brushed my teeth or washed. Tasks completed, I left, half walking, half running up to the village centre. When I got to the town hall, the men had lined up in rows with the "tanks" parked to one side. A church service had just ended, and the vicar addressed the men from a makeshift pulpit set up on the village hall front porch. He wished them good luck.

An order rang out, "Attention. Right turn. Dismiss." The men gathered into small groups. Men wearing white doctorlike coats handed out red ribbons, which the home guard tied on their right arms. Group by group the men dispersed through the village.

I watched two of the "tanks" being positioned on the bridge. The turret of one pointed diagonally across the river upstream and one pointed straight across the bridge. Men fixed water-filled rubber balloons, made of knotted-up inner tubes, along the bridge.

When I noticed movement on the house roofs farther up the river, I realized men had positioned themselves with their legs straddling the smaller chimney pots. Someone shouted from ground level to the roof of the village hall. A man on the roof signaled with flags in semaphore. A second man shouted information down to ground level, and a white-coated man wearing a green sash with the word umpire on it sat at a table and relayed information. A military gentleman shouted instructions back. The semaphore man, who was apparently the focal point for information, signaled sequentially around the village.

During a spell of inactivity, I wandered down to the bridge to see if anything was happening there. One of the "tank" crew said I could watch but I had to stand in a doorway. Five minutes later, he came over and suggested I go upstairs in the adjacent shop and watch from the upstairs window. From there, I had a good view of the bridge and parts of the road over the other side of the bridge running upstream. The roads appeared deserted. Women in doorways and windows waited and watched.

For a long while, nothing happened. Then I caught sight of movement. Upstream, a column moved quickly. It disappeared behind trees and houses. I shouted to the men below that I'd seen movement. They bade me be quiet.

I heard rumbling that sounded like people running. Houses screened the road by the river, so I couldn't see the near end of it. Around the corner came a herd of forty or fifty cows at full speed. They turned and headed for the bridge. The cows in front tried to stop when they saw the "tanks," but the ones to the rear pushed them on. None of the arm waving by the men manning the tanks made any difference. The cows thundered over the bridge past the tanks into the village centre.

Minutes later, an out-of-breath, well-built lady in Wellingtons and a long coat tied up with baling string followed. She swore and cursed. She had been taking the cows back to the fields after milking while her husband was out on "these stupid maneuvers." She'd nearly got to the field gate when a steam-driven road roller came full speed around the corner and blasted the trumpet horn. "It sounded like a ship birthing," she said. "With camouflage paint, flags flying, blue bunting, and clothes posts sticking out the front. It sure scared the hell out of me and my cows."

A home guard calmed her and told her it was an enemy "tank." "Ours have red bunting," he said, pointing to the tractors.

She nodded but still seemed bewildered. "What do I do about my cows?" she asked.

They told her they'd round them up and bring them back to her later in the morning. She wasn't happy, but she accepted their reassurances and continued walking into town, talking to herself and shrugging her shoulders.

We heard the rumble of the steamroller coming. It turned the corner at the end of the bridge and let off scarecrow charges as the steamroller started to cross. Whoosh! The rubber balloons split, sending out a cascade of diluted lime wash over the bridge. Scarecrow charges let off either side of the bridge, followed by silence.

Out of the doorway across the road, a man wearing a white coat, an umpire, appeared. Another appeared over the other side of the bridge. They met in the middle and compared notes. The villagers won that encounter.

The steamroller, covered in chalk dust, indicated hits from dummy grenades thrown off the houses roofs. The lime wash covering the bridge meant the bridge had been blown up with the steamroller on it. Another victory for the village.

The man operating the steamroller and the dozen or so following on foot had their blue armbands removed and were marched up the road to the village hall. I decided to go back to the farmyard to see if Owen had returned. Passing the village square, I saw that the cows had been rounded up and were standing quietly in from of the town hall. On my way to Mrs. Davies's house, I saw more cows standing in the river, drinking.

The farmyard was deserted, but I could hear crow scarers going off in the distance. I climbed a willow tree by the wooden bridge running over the river and managed to get high up, where I had a partial view up and down the river as well as a view over the farmyard, the fields, and the land running down the side of the farm.

I noticed movement in the bushes down the river from me. Men had weeds draped over their heads, and I saw flashes of red armbands, so I knew they were ours. In the distance, I saw men wading up the river. The ambush worked. The men with the blue armbands got past the camouflaged pocket before our men surprised them. I learned the Home Guard had been preparing the ambush for a week. All they wanted was for soldiers to come up the river. The men walked up the bank to the road and headed for the village centre.

As they passed, I saw movement in the top field. Creeping and crawling from tree to tree and amongst the pigs were half a dozen men. Three or four ran, bent over, down the hedgerow. They reached the gate first and observed the farmyard and inspected the buildings before tossing in dummy hand grenades. Satisfied that the yard was clear, they waved to the men in the field to join them, all half crouching behind the stone wall, and headed for the farmyard entrance.

Three cracks rang out. I knew that sound. It was the double discharge of twelve bore shotguns. I peered into the farmyard through the blue haze. Heads and shoulders appeared from within the moldy hay on top of the corner dung pile. One was Owen, still sucking his pipe. They had fired into the air, but a few of the blue-ribboned men clutched their chest, feigning a heart attack. Owen and his colleagues rounded up the blue ribbons, and a white-coated umpire came out of a barn with a scorecard in hand.

I climbed down and joined the men and discovered that Owen and his friends weren't supposed to discharge their twelve bores. They were only supposed to make a noise. They waited for the umpire to pronounce the verdict. Owen appeared unperturbed. He just smiled and puffed on his pipe. The fun was over for that day.

Chapter 5

BULLY FOR JOHN

Autumn came quickly. Leaves turned a profusion of russets, yellows, and browns. Flowers died back, and garden lawns stayed long and damp. The river gradually changed from a slow-moving, meandering stream into a stormy flow, rising perceptibly every day.

For a week, I kept busy with my farmyard jobs and helping Mrs. Davies bottle fruit and wash and stalk plums, gooseberries, and black currants. Also, I worked in the playroom on school exercises from books Mrs. Davies got for me.

News from the war front was grim. The country was in a state of readiness, not knowing what Hitler was planning and assuming the worst. Uplifting news of factory output in armaments came through regularly on the radio. Announcers urged workers to keep it up and emphasized the workers' contribution to the war effort and the essential role they played in defeating Hitler. The radio engendered a spirit of total unity and determination by playing uplifting music and sentimental songs for sweethearts. Comedy programmes aired in which Hitler or the Jerries were the butts of scurrilous jokes. The radio was totally immersed in morale boosting.

There was a slant on bad news. If the Luftwaffe had bombed the hell out of a city, their bombs had missed vital targets. A factory that had been hit was back in operation in four days. Reports of thousands of women and children maimed, killed, or homeless were played down. Emphasis was put on the heroic efforts of the firefighter, rescue, and ambulance teams. The number of aircraft shot down was minimal, and they were in reality a small number relative to the size and strength of the Luftwaffe, whose factories were well geared up for production. Although, according to the radio, our factory output was quickly surpassing the loss due to attrition, the workers of the country were encouraged to feel proud. Much of the praise was directed at women, who had been called upon—and had more than met the challenge—to run the production lines.

America's reluctance to pitch into the war was criticized in the news. We bought or leased armaments and food from the USA, but U-boats made life at sea perilous causing huge losses in shipping. The British Isles had to be prepared for a future assault on mainland Europe and keep the shipping lanes open for essential armament and food supplies, daunting tasks. "Dig for Victory" was the slogan. Everyone with a spare piece of ground was encouraged to grow food with more and more emphasis put on agriculture. Our food supplies were drying up.

The news on the Western Front wasn't encouraging. Joe Stalin had been caught napping by placing too much faith in Hitler's word and a nonaggression pact. The Luftwaffe knocked a huge part of the Russian air force in the first twenty-four hours of the assault in June. It had taken out much of them on the ground. The radio reported figures as high as 80 percent losses of Russian planes. In three months, the Germans swept through eastern Russia. Leningrad to the north and Stalingrad to the south were under siege. Columns of troops made fast progress on their push to Moscow.

The one piece of good news was that the German assault on Russia relieved pressure on the British Isles. The frequency of night bombing raids dropped dramatically, but continued often enough to remind us we were in a war. Targets were more often selected for their strategic value. Docks and armament factories were under siege.

Over the gooseberries, Mrs. Davies informed me I was going to start school. The village children had gone back a week before. The headmistress planned to filter the evacuees into the school system.

"A lady is coming to see you in the afternoon to assess your scholastic abilities," Mrs. Davies told me. I was to show her the books I worked from and some of my writing. She might give me a short arithmetic test.

After hearing that, concentrating on the gooseberries became impossible. Doubts grew in my mind. School? How would I fare? How would I fit it? What about my freedom to do as I pleased? Two hours of study a day in the front playroom was more than enough. At times, Mrs. Davies was a hard taskmaster. Well, at least, I'd meet some other boys. Now and again, I felt lonely.

The lady who came that afternoon was the headmistress of the local school. When she arrived, I had a pleasant surprise because she was the lady who'd been in the train carriage on the way to Talgarth. She recognized me and put me at ease instantly. I was to call her Mrs. Evans. She knew my family background, what my mother and father were doing, and where my sister was. I told her I'd started school three times, the longest period being at the chapel. She asked me questions and got me talking about the subjects we had covered.

She gave me three books to read from, each one more difficult. She helped me with words in the most difficult book, but she said I'd done well. The arithmetic did not go so well. Adding and subtracting were fine, but I had difficulty with division and multiplication. Disaster would be a better word for my knowledge of division and multiplication.

My map books sat on the table, so I showed her Europe and pointed out the various countries as she told me their names. She was impressed when I showed her where Dunkirk was, as well as Leningrad and Stalingrad. When we talked about Africa and South America, I told her about the people and animals there. I even told her about Chalky and his geographic books.

Mrs. Evans assured me I was going to do fine and that I should start school on Monday at nine o'clock sharp. She said the school provided meals and milk break in the morning, but I needed to take a cup or jam jar.

The next Monday came quickly. The school was a small Victorian steep-roofed stone building. The entrance was across an ample asphalt playground. The school and playground were divided into girls and boys. The left hand side was for boys; the right for girls. Children up to about twelve years old attended.

Once inside the building, I met Miss Jones, my teacher. I sat at a table with five other boys. We stood for prayers before lessons began. We singsonged our multiplication tables after prayers. I was all right through the sevens but kept quiet after that. Miss Jones set out exercises and then came around as we put up our hands.

Talking when we should have been working was a crime. Miss Jones had a kind but sharp tongue, and I soon learnt to be quiet. The ultimate threat, after being put at a table alone and then standing in the corner facing the wall, was to be sent to see Mrs. Evans. The students feared her even more than Miss Jones. Two visits to the corner were enough for me. I sat at the desk and copied what was going on off the other boys—my tablemates were ahead of me—and kept quiet. Miss Jones soon cottoned on to what was happening and repositioned me at a desk with four boys, right under her nose. For weeks, she gave us a disproportionate amount of her time.

Miss Jones wrote ten words on the blackboard every morning, and we wrote them down as she emphasized the meaning. The next day, she'd write ten more words on the board. Then she asked a boy the meaning of a word or the spelling from the previous day's list. She pinned a league table to the wall with marks given for correct answers. At first, I fared badly, but then I wrote the words out and studied them during the day. I soon climbed up the league table. By first term's end, I was back at a normal table.

Writing and arithmetic were the main core lessons interspersed with painting, drawing, and identification of plants and trees—at which I excelled—and the basic history of the British Isles. The day finished with Miss Jones reading from a book: Just William, Tom Sawyer, Brer Rabbit, Aesop's Fables, and Greek mythology.

Life in the playground got off to a bad start. I had only been at school a few days when an older boy decided he wanted my father's cap badge that I wore pinned to my jumper. He tried to barter apples and a penknife for it, but I refused to part with it. He tried to pick a fight by calling me names, "Cockney bum" or "yellow." I walked away, but he came up and pushed me in the back, taunting me. Finally, I lost my temper and went for him, arms flailing. I soon wished I'd left him alone because within seconds, I was in a wrestling hold, flat on my back, out of breath. He sat on top of me and took the cap badge off my jumper. As he got up, I went for him again, only to end up on the asphalt with a smarting nose. I got up, determined to have a third try, but two older boys—I recognized them from the train journey to Talgarth—held me back.

They half-carried, half-frog-marched me away from the bully and his group of friends to the wall surrounding the playground. "If you're going to fight," said the taller boy, "you'd better know how. At the moment, you're just setting yourself up for a pasting."

"The cap badge," I panted.

"We know. We watched what was going on." They both wore cap badges.

"I want it back," I said. "He's stolen it."

"You won't get it back by fighting," said the shorter boy. "Not the way you fight, anyhow."

"I'll go and tell the teacher then," I said.

They both gasped. "Things are bad enough in the playground and around the village as it is. There are more of them than us. Some boys resent us being here. We don't know why, but it has to do with the Welsh and the English."

"But there's a bloody war on," I said, still fuming.

"Don't make much difference to some lads," said the short boy. "We're different. We speak differently."

The boys introduced themselves. The taller one was Jed, big for his age. The shorter boy, who did the most talking, was Stan. They'd come from a large estate on the edge of Epsom across the commons from where I lived.

"Listen," Stan said, "the only way you can get the cap badge back is to take it the way he got it. The boy's a damn right bully and gets away with these things. He's got a brother in our class who's not much better." Stan turned to Jed and said, "You could take after the big brother, if it came to it."

"Not a problem," Jed said with confidence.

"How old are you?" Stan asked.

"Coming on eight," I said.

Stan felt my arms. "Tall and well built for your age," he said. "I thought you was older. I think we can do something with you. Meet us in the playground tomorrow at lunchtime."

At lunchtime for the next three weeks, we slipped out the rear gate and walked a short way up to a field out of sight of the school. Stan and Jed put me through my paces. I learnt how to block lefts and rights, to lead the left with the chin, and to come in with the right, three buttons up into the solar plexus.

"That's where you'll get him," Stan said. "Don't hit his head. You'll hurt your hand. A straight arm, flat hand up underneath the nose is far more certain and just as effective."

I even learnt how to rabbit-punch to the back of the neck in case we got to wrestling.

"Don't forget his balls," Jed said. "If in difficulty, just grab him and hang on for dear life. He'll let go of you quick enough."

The third week, we spent thumping into a straw bale left over in the field. I had hankies wrapped around my hands and came in weaving and ducking while Stan and Jed held up the bale. In between times, Stan would spar and wrestle with me. "Watch the hands," he kept saying. "Now right, right again."

I grabbed his balls in one session, and he let out a yell. "Good," he said, giving me a back elbow, something new to add to my arsenal.

I gained confidence even though I was exhausted after each session and knew in a few more weeks, I'd risk taking on Hue, the bully.

It hadn't occurred to me that I hadn't been in a fight before or that the real thing might be something different. I spent the weekends pummeling the haystacks in the farmyard barn. Owen caught me at it and asked me what I was about. I told him.

"Yes," he said. "I have heard there's been some minor problems, not easy to stop. Boys will be boys. The occasional flare-up is to be expected. It was the same when I was young," he added. "I could come up to the school and get your badge for you, but I don't think it would solve any problems. Might make them worse. I'm afraid, young man, you're going to have to learn to look out for yourself. As they say, either put up or shut up. What do you think your father would say?"

"Possibly the same," I said. "But I haven't spoken to him for a long time. GranDad would say the bully needs a bayonet up the Khyber Pass." It was one of his favorite expressions.

Owen laughed and nodded in agreement.

My resolve to put matters right grew daily, and the moment came sooner than expected—during milk and playtime break Monday morning. I finished my milk and headed out to the playground to join Stan and Jed and other evacuees I'd palled up with. I got a smack on the back of the head.

"Come on, move yourself." It was Hue. His cronies followed him out of the doorway. He wore my cap badge and two others that he'd bullied away from others.

I saw red. Anger welled inside me. I turned around and rushed at him with my arms out and gave him an almighty shove. He went backward through his cronies, tripped, and ended up flat on his back.

I took a few paces back and stood with my hands ready. I wasn't backing off. Hue got up and brushed himself down. His classmates sniggered. His eyes were wild, and I swore the nostrils on his large, fat face enlarged. I'd seen a raging bull, and he looked like one.

He came running at me, his hands raised at the ready. I stood my ground. I blocked the first right and turned as his left came over, grazing me on the head. Hue went past me with the momentum of his attack. He came in again, arms swinging. I ducked and weaved, moving backward all the time, taking most of his blows to my arms. One or two got through to my head, but I managed to ride the force of them. Hue knew how to fight and throw a punch, but could he take one? I hadn't yet landed a punch. I was only able to feign, threaten, move side to side, and take a step at a time backwards.

Hue stood back, weighed me up with his left, and took an almighty swipe at me with his right. He swung around with his shoulders behind it.

It was a haymaker. The momentum of the punch propelled him forward as fist and arm swung in an arc.

I saw my chance, possibly my only one. I crouched and dropped my right shoulder. I put my left hand up to parry the punch and brought my clenched right hand up from my knees, putting my back and shoulder into it. His right hand flew over my head. As it did, my right buried itself in the top half of his stomach, just below the rib cage. He folded up like a jackknife. His head came down and met my knee coming up. He left the ground for a split second, hanging horizontally. The bully ended up dazed, lying flat on the playground asphalt.

I spun around with my fists still raised. I had no need to bother. Nobody else wanted to get involved.

Jed gave me a pat on the back. "Touch and go for a moment," he said. "Boy, what a right! Don't think anybody else will push you around." He was right.

Stan unpinned the cap badges off Hue's jumper. He gave me mine, and two other willing hands asked for theirs. Hue came out of his daze and sat up groggily. Two classmates helped him up and took him into the cloakroom to wash his face.

I had a cut lip and felt my right eye swelling. However, I was already healing inside. I felt a real sense of justice. A few lads came up and patted me on the back, most of them village lads. Hue wasn't well liked.

Miss Evans was not the nice lady I had come to know. She summoned me to her study later in the day. Hue had gone home with his injuries. She wanted to know everything. He told her that I had given him a good hiding and didn't bother to explain why. I was reluctant to tell her anything except that it was true: I had fought Hue. My eye and lip were living proof. She pressed me hard, said I was a hooligan and she wouldn't tolerate hooliganism in her school. It wasn't the behavior she'd come to expect from her boys. She was considering expelling me and told me to return to my classroom. She would see me later.

I sat in the classroom under the watchful eye of Miss Jones. She didn't appear to approve of me either.

Stuff them, I thought. Let them believe what they like. I know the truth.

An hour later, Mrs. Evans summoned me again to her study. This time, she was more pleasant. "Right," she said. "I have got to the bottom of the affair. It seems Hue stole your cap badge."

"And others," I said.

"Yes, I have that as well. It also appears he's been throwing his weight around. Still, it's not a reason to half-kill him. The war is bad enough as it is. Why didn't you come to me or another teacher?"

I told her what Jed said about telling tales. She assured me that the teachers were my friends and I could confide in them.

"There are ways and means of obtaining justice without putting anyone on the spot," she told me.

I wasn't sure what she meant, but she instilled confidence in me. She asked about my mother, father, and sister. She wondered how I was finding school. We talked a bit longer, and I promised it wouldn't happen again and agreed to shake hands with Hue when he returned to school, the next day, as it happened.

Hue must have received a ticking off too because he came and found me and shook my hand. "Good fight," he said through a split lip. "Now let's be friends." And that's the way it was. He must have had more pressure put on him than I had.

In my heart, I was prepared to fight him again if the need arose even though I would have thought twice about letting Mrs. Evans down.

Later in the day, Mrs. Evans visited each classroom with a handful of pictures of blitzed London. She gave figures of the homeless, deaths, and other casualties. She told what the evacuees had been through and said the school should make us welcome. It worked. I was the centre of attention for days as I answered questions about the bombing and evacuation. From that day forward, nobody questioned that I—or, for that matter, any of the evacuees—wasn't part of the school or the village.

The autumn days moved into winter. The trees lost their leaves, and dark clouds hung around forever. Frequent rainy days caused the river to rise several feet and move swiftly. The hard-packed farmyard turned into soft, oozing mud.

Early December was my eighth birthday, but it was more memorable for other reasons.

First, the news came that Japan bombed Pearl Harbor. The USA declared war on Japan. A day later came the news that Germany and Italy sided with Japan. Churchill announced that the United Kingdom aligned with the United States and was now at war with Japan.

I thought we had enough on our plate, but I supposed Churchill knew what he was doing. Anyhow, Hitler had to face Russia, the USA, and the United Kingdom and Commonwealth.

I remembered Chalky's words, "He won't stand a chance." It was a clear insight, but it was far from easy. The real war hadn't started yet. Hitler had done as he pleased so far. The tide turned slowly but inevitably, just as Chalky had predicted. Hitler didn't have the manpower or resources to fight on three fronts, even with the Italians' help. He was going to find out over the next three years.

The first crack in Hitler's invincibility came with the news of a Russian offensive. The German army was ill equipped for the severe Russian winter. They had bogged down. The Russians were coming back at them. News came in of a massive battle at Stalingrad. Casualties were in the hundreds of thousands, but Hitler had met with his first reversal of fortune. The Russians pushed the Germans back, and Hitler's domination was on the wane. This news was infectious. People around me spoke with confidence.

Mr. Davies and their younger son came home for a few days at Christmas. As a surprise to Mrs. Davies, their eldest son and daughter turned up for a forty-eight-hour visit. They looked very smart, he in his RAF uniform and she in an army-nursing uniform. They were stationed in the Midlands somewhere and, judging by the conversation, had both been heavily involved in the war.

We had goose for Christmas dinner, which meant one less in the farmyard. After dinner, the conversation turned to the war. The USA joining in and Russia's push were the focal points. The RAF had been trying to ferry supplies and food to the besieged city of Leningrad. Aeroplane losses had been heavy.

Mrs. Davies's elder son showed us pictures of airmen posing in front of their planes. The most startling pictures were of Coventry, or what was left of it. I'd seen bombed-out areas, but nothing like that. The intensity of the bombing wiped out a whole city. Mrs. Davies's son flew that night on convoy escort duty. The aircrew saw Coventry burning from over a hundred miles away.

A parcel containing two hand-knitted jumpers and a letter arrived from Mother over Christmas. There was also a letter from Dad to Mrs. Davies. He said Mother had been quite ill but was on the road to recovery. My father hadn't passed on this news before because he didn't want to worry me. He was trying to organize a leave so he could come down and see my sister and me. Although the bombing had quieted down, they thought I should stay where I was for the present. He sent a picture of himself in uniform, which I put beside my bed with great pride.

I perked up at the news that Dad might come to see me but was worried about Mother. I pressed Mrs. Davies for more news. She said I was going to have another brother or sister, but there had been complications with the pregnancy and Mother had lost the child. It had left her weak, and she required hospitalization. The worst was over. She was at home now, and the two capable nurses living with her were looking after her.

Talk in the living room turned to news of family and friends, marriages, babies, and engagements. I felt lonely in a room full of people and excused myself, saying I wanted to see what was going on in the farmyard. I put on my coat and wandered off through the farmyard and up to the top field.

"Damn the war," I said to myself over and over. "Damn Hitler, the bastard. Just wish I was old enough to fight him myself." I couldn't get Mother out of my head. Although I'd suffered bouts of homesickness before, this time was the worst. It was Christmas Day after all.

I thought back to the Christmases I could remember and the family gatherings, chatter, toys, and laughter. Leaning against an apple tree, I barely noticed the fine drizzle or the fading light. I felt sick in my head, sick in my stomach. I felt physically ill and wanted to be sick but couldn't.

I was so preoccupied that I didn't notice a lone figure walking toward me. It was Owen with shotgun crooked under his arm. He startled me when he spoke. "Thought it was you," he said. "Everything all right?" When he saw my face, he knelt down beside me, put his hands on my shoulders, and held me square to him. Looking straight at me, he said, "Come on, John. Tell me. Tell Owen. What's the problem?"

"You can't help." I shook my head. "It's no real problem. Just how I feel inside."

"Homesick, are we, lad? Understandable."

I nodded. Homesick seemed the right word, an intangible. No reason. Nothing one could put right. Just thoughts flowing from my head to my stomach, pushing each time farther into the stomach and robbing me of any resilience to fight the emptiness. I felt a void that needed to be filled with love and affection.

"You have friends here, you know," Owen said.

I nodded. I did have friends, some very good friends.

Owen put an arm around me and pulled me to him and tousled my hair. It felt good to be hugged. The tension inside me eased. Owen understood. Nothing needed to be said. He took my hand, and we walked down the field together.

"Come on," he said. "Come with me to the piggery. A sow had a litter this morning."

The warm yellow light over the mother sow, the dozen piglets snuggling up to her teats, and the straw around them reminded me of the pictures I'd seen of Mary and Joseph on Christmas cards and the stories Miss Jones read us at school before Christmas break.

"Twelve," Owen said. "On Christmas Day. Now which one shall we call John? That one, I think." He pointed. "He can be Mark." He pointed to another. "And that one Matthew." He went through the names of the disciples. "That little bugger out on his own can be Judas."

I looked at Owen. "Some might be sows," I said.

"Well, I'm not going to call a pig Mary," he said. "That would be pushing luck too far."

I laughed with him. I felt better.

Di and David were home from boarding school for Christmas although I didn't see much of them until after Christmas Day because they had to get their prep out of the way. I gathered this was posh talk for homework, something I had to do over the holidays too and hadn't yet got around to. No doubt, I'd get a firm reminder from Mrs. Davies.

Stan and Jed came around to see me most days, and Mrs. Davies allowed them in to play billiards. Sometimes Di and David joined us. We'd walk around the farm, over the fields, and through the woods, firing off catapults at anything that moved. We liked to heave cardboard boxes off the wooden bridge into the fast-moving river, trying to sink the boxes with the catapult before they got out of range.

School came around soon enough. There was a last-minute rush to get my homework done. Mrs. Davies helped me. She did most of it. I think Miss Jones thought so too. "All your own work next time, please," she wrote on my papers.

Stan turned up for school on Friday morning obviously in pain. He never said much about where he lived, and I'd never been to see him where he was billeted. He said he hadn't done well enough that morning and the man he lived with gave him a good belting. By lunchtime, Stan was still feeling uncomfortable and seemed very down, which was unusual for him. Usually, he was the talkative one, always cheering up other people.

"I've got to get away," he said. "I can't take anymore."

"Any more of what?" we asked.

Stan told us that every morning before school, he had to put in two hours of damned hard work, preparing the hash, feeding the pigs, chopping wood, carrying pails of milk, and other chores. He had a hurried breakfast and went off to school. After school, he followed a similar routine. "The missus is all right," he said. "She tries to look after me. But him! That bastard is always short-tempered. He throws his hands around, gives his wife a belt now and again, and if I do anything wrong, there's a lot of shouting. If I'm not quick, I get his big hand around my head. Damn well hurts, I tell you. He justifies this by repeating, 'Got to earn your keep, boy. Got to earn your keep.' It's just plain slave labor." Stan paused before he repeated, "I tell you, I've got to get away."

"Look," he said. "I'll show you what happened this morning." He took off his jacket and pulled up his sweater and shirt. Three weals stood out on his back, blue in the middle and flaming red on the outside. "I tripped over the feeding bucket he left lying around. Me and the two milk pails I was carrying flew across the dairy floor. Nearly knocked myself out. Before I could get up, he flew into a rage and took off his leather belt and flew into me. He called me a twerp and a clumsy little bastard, saying, 'I'll teach you. Milk is money.'

"I half-crawled and half-ran back to the farmhouse, changed clothes, grabbed what I could off the breakfast table, and came to school. I'm not looking forward to going back tonight." He shook his head. "Somehow, I must get away."

We pooled ideas as to what he should do. None of us had money with us. We weren't quite sure how he would be received if he came home with one of us. We'd have to ask first. I said he could stay in the hay barn in the igloo we'd built. I could smuggle food out to him. We debated at length. Other boys said they would find food and smuggle out the odd blanket.

Stan was afraid of being discovered and taken back. He'd written to his mother, but he was sure the letters hadn't been posted. He didn't even get a letter over Christmas.

After looking at the options, we all agreed the barn idea was the best. Some of us had saved pocket money at home. If Stan stayed in the barn overnight, we could find out how much we had between us. Hopefully, we'd find enough for his train fare home. Trains weren't running regularly, and nobody had a clue what the fare would be. Stan was obviously terrified about returning to his billeting.

Owen might help, and Mrs. Davies surely would, but would I be burdening them with a problem they weren't in a position to sort out? Instinct told me they would help, but I had another idea forming. It would be an act of faith. Dare I try it? I kept the idea to myself until after the dinner break. If it went wrong, Stan might be worse off. How, I didn't know. Grown-ups tended to stick together. However, how could the weals on Stan's back be explained away? I had to have faith, to believe what I was told. I mulled over my new idea for the first twenty minutes of the afternoon lessons.

I put my hand up and asked to be excused to go to the toilet. Miss Jones said something about sorting myself out at lunchtime, but she excused me. I went down the hall passageway and knocked on Mrs. Evans's door. When no one answered, I opened the door, but she wasn't there. My confidence waned. I turned around as a classroom door opened down the way, and there she was. She saw me, gave a quick smile, and asked why I was out of my classroom.

"An act of faith," I said.

She motioned me into her study.

I told her everything: what happened to Stan, our plans to help, and how terrified Stan was. I asked if she could help.

When her face turned from a concentrated frown to anger, I figured I was in trouble, but she promised she would get matters put right and took me back to my class. She explained to Miss Jones that she had detained me and thanked me for coming to see her. She said she would speak to me after school.

I felt Stan's problem was in good hands, but I was still nervous, thinking about the outcome.

As I was going out to play, I noticed the village police sergeant and a man in a suit in the school corridor and figured they came because of Stan. I hoped Stan told us everything and hadn't been up to any mischief. No, I thought, consoling myself. He's genuine enough.

Stan was missing during the break. Jed said Mrs. Evans came into their classroom and asked to see him, and he hadn't returned.

"Hope he isn't in more trouble," Jed said.

I didn't think he was but didn't say anything.

Before break time finished, a flustered large man came striding across the playground. I would have recognized that scowling face anywhere. He was the man I'd poked my tongue at on the night of my arrival in Talgarth. He was even wearing the same clothes.

At the end of lessons, Miss Jones asked me to stay behind. She said Mrs. Evans wanted to see me. I wandered around the classroom and looked out the window in time to see the bluff farmer leaving with the police sergeant.

A few minutes later, I saw Stan leaving with a lady and gentleman. They were deep in conversation.

Not long after, Mrs. Evans entered the classroom. Her face creased in a large smile. "All sorted out," she said. "Stan has a new home with some very nice people, just up the road from the school. I've seen Jed. He'll tell your friends not to worry. A policeman is going to get Stan's belongings. Stan should have no more problems with that man." She paused. "Thank you for coming to see me."

"Was the man who left with the policeman the one Stan was staying with?" I asked.

"Yes," she said. "A nasty piece of work if ever I saw one. He hasn't been in the village long and deserves more than the stern reprimand he got from the police sergeant. He tried to lie his way out of it by saying he hadn't seen Stan this morning, and then Stan must have got the marks falling over. He even said Stan was lying. The doctor and police sergeant weren't fooled one bit. And neither was I." She paused. "A nasty piece of work," she repeated. "I pity his poor wife."

The vibrations and chemistry I'd felt from that man were accurate. My instant dislike for him was justified. I'd had a close shave.

"Now you should be off home," Mrs. Evans said. "Before Mrs. Davies worries about you."

Chapter 6

ENCORE! ENCORE!

The hedgerows threw off the doldrums of winter. Early spring arrived, heralded by snowdrops, crocuses, and primroses, as the hedgerows passed into an accelerated welcome of new life. Tulips followed masses of daffodils. Catkins on the hazel trees gave way to light green shoots and leaves. Azaleas burst forth, racing the lilacs into bloom. Rhododendrons swelled up in bud, waiting for the warmer days of May. The hedgerows came alive with chatter as birds went about their nesting. Farmyard chickens brooded and had to be shooed off their eggs. Bulling by cows in the field indicated sap rising everywhere.

The days got longer and warmer. Rains of late March and early April had swollen the river into a thick brown torrent that ebbed back quickly as the warmer and drier days of late April and May came in, ushering in a flaming June.

I took to roaming the surrounding countryside, exploring paths, marveling at the size of the foxgloves, thick platoons of them standing to attention. Bluebells matted the woods upstream, making a thick carpet impossible to walk through without damaging them. I gathered a bunch for Mrs. Davies, who, although delighted, instructed me to nip them off and leave a piece of stalk. Pulling the stalk from the bulb left them blind, never to appear again.

The meadows came alive with lambs. It was fun to watch their antics. I came across a fox stalking through the grass with four cubs trailing her. The vixen stopped, gave me an inquisitive stare, and carried on walking at an unhurried pace. Rabbits romped everywhere, especially in the morning. I'd found ten, fifteen, or twenty, with young, in a glade or clearing in the woods, oblivious to danger. Now and again, I came across the usually nocturnal badger, scurrying off, its rear end unmistakably bobbing up and down as it propelled itself forward.

Grass snakes were harmless but unpleasant if I came upon them suddenly. If I tapped the ground with a stick or my foot, they'd slither away, disappearing into the hedgerow unless it was mealtime. I shuddered at seeing a frog half-swallowed—a ghastly sight—and squealing a high-pitched squeal to the last as the grass snake worked its jaws until the frog disappeared.

Occasionally, I found knitting-wool bundles of aspiring grass snakes on the edge of ponds, the bundles heaving with their heads sticking out from the self-made wool. About the size of large worms, the young ones made no attempt to untangle themselves from one another.

In the ponds, the moorhens, coot, and wild duck eggs were easy prey. I took off my Wellies to wade among the grasses and reeds and fill my pockets for a fine breakfast. I found clutches of up to eight eggs. Owen, on his trips with me, told me to take only one or two from each nest. "Want some for next year," he said.

His words didn't stop him from taking a pot with his shotgun at any wild duck or geese that flew nearby. "Never shoot at a sitting duck," he instructed. "Get them flying first. Gives them a sporting chance. Anyhow, they sink in the water and are difficult to find." Noble or practical, Owen's philosophy was unto himself. He usually had two opinions on any problem, task, or difficulty: the way it might be done, and his way, easily justified. There was no point arguing with him. He could be quite stubborn. His dad and GranDad had done it that way, and it was as the good Lord intended.

My rambling took me farther and farther afield. At weekends on returning from the farm after milking and after eating a large breakfast, I wrapped up leftovers that I carried in a brown paper bag and help myself to an apple from the larder. I wandered off over the fields or up and down the river. I met other farmers or farmworkers I knew in their fields and stopped to chat, share their lunches, or have a mug of tea poured from a tin flask.

Mrs. Davies was happy for me to go off wandering. She didn't mind as long as I was back by teatime and was careful of the river although the river by now had died down to a brisk meandering. I often took a fishing rod Mrs. Davies found so I could fish the eddy pools on the corners of the river as it turned and wound through the countryside. I was never very successful, but fishing was a pleasant way to spend an afternoon.

Stan and Jed came with me sometimes although they both had regular weekend jobs on farms, which they enjoyed and got paid for. They were soon to leave Talgarth to join a work camp where they would mix in education and working on the land.

On one of those glorious early June days—the sun full and shining out of a cloudless sky, the air warm and fresh, full of the aroma of plants and flowers, the air filled with bird sounds and memories of the past winter with its sunless days, heavy clouds and constant drizzle faded—I decided to explore farther upriver.

Setting off over the stone bridge in the village centre, I headed out through the village over a wooden bridge that crossed the meandering river. I walked up the hill and climbed over a fence opposite the cottage hospital into a field where I helped pick mushrooms in September. The field led down to the river's edge. Here the river had gently sloped banks where cattle could drink. Farther on, there were glades full of flowers.

I climbed over stiles, situated so that one could walk from field to field without leaving a gate open. I came upon a lone fisherman and stopped for a chat. "Oh yes," he said. "You're the lad staying with Mrs. Davies."

I didn't know him, but he knew who I was.

Two hours into my journey, I began to think I'd walked far enough. My legs needed rest. I hadn't come across a fisherman for over half an hour. I came to a glade where the river turned gently away. A large flat rock jutted out into the river. I decided to sit there to eat my sandwiches and drink from the river.

I laid flat on the rock and peered into a deep pool beneath me, where large trout barely moved, just flashing their tail fins to hold themselves against the current. They might have been having a midday nap, spoiled by my dropping a stone into the pool. When the ripples died, the trout had disappeared.

After I finished my sandwiches, I soaked up the sun until a sound coming from upriver intruded upon the rippling river sounds and the chat of birds, and I decided to investigate.

The wooded slopes lining the river ran into a well-used path that descended down through the trees and turned to follow alongside the riverbank. The noise, a low rumble, grew in volume as I followed the path. To my surprise, as I rose up over a brow of the footpath, I found my first waterfall.

I sat at the crest of the rise with my elbows on my knees and my hands to my face, staring at it. It was magnificent, but also frightening as so much power unleashed before my eyes.

It must have been thirty feet high or even higher. The water fell into a deep dark pool, creating turbulence and a trough wave that flowed across the pool to large boulders acting as a dam. As the water flowed between the boulders, it turned white, cascaded down, and formed rapids as the water level lowered a farther five feet. The river gradually smoothed out until it reached where I sat and became a smooth, inviting flow.

Three tributaries—one larger one to the left and two smaller ones to the right—fed the top of the waterfall. They spread out as they left their respective ledges to meet halfway down and produce a wall of water eighteen feet wide. The water funneled into the pool by steep almost vertical sides of rock carved out in bygone ages. Between the two tributaries to the right was a young tree in full leaf surrounded at the base by a large clump of maidenhead ferns. The ferns trailed down the side, providing a fragile boundary between the two tributaries. Bright sunlight made its way through the tree branches that lined each side of the pool, producing a magical rainbow that rose in a crescent from either side and across the front of the flowing wall.

I sat for about five minutes, taking in the scene before venturing nearer. As I came close to the pool, the proportions appeared to enlarge. A strong sense of danger overcame me. I was so close to something so beautiful and yet so powerful, so close to a power that would surely take my life if I were to fall in the pool.

The riverbank had eroded, creating a slope. I managed to negotiate the slope easily and stepped onto the first boulder. After giving thought to jumping across to the next boulder, I decided the risk was too great and sat down with my feet just above the frothing water. I took in nature's display and gradually grew more confident and at ease with my discovery.

There was a spiritual presence, an eerie feeling of a presence that wasn't earthly, similar to the feeling I got in the small corrugated-tin church back near my house at Epsom. I had a sense of not being alone. Don't be silly, I thought. Your imagination is playing tricks on you. It's only water flowing over a ledge, even if it is spectacular.

The fine mist above the surging trough played in the sunlight, producing miniature rainbows that held only for seconds. After sitting on the rock and taking in the scene, I decided not to venture any farther, knowing it was time to return home. It must have been coming into early afternoon.

I was about to leave when I caught sight of a butterfly that alighted on the next rock. It opened and closed its wings, showing the dark brown underneath and a predominantly orange upper surface. It had brown flecks and brown, white, and blue circles on each wing, similar to markings on our aircraft and had a wingspan of four to five inches.

As I sat riveted on my rock, it did an amazing thing. It took off and flew into the edge of the waterfall's rising mist, fluttered up to the front edge of the falling water and, in an erratic motion, moved up and down and side to side, just in front of the cascade, a sort of ritual or dance. Then it came back to the rock and rested before repeating the performance, a solo performance just for me.

I had no idea how long it danced its second performance, but I couldn't take my eyes off it. I convinced myself it was dancing to music. I was sure of it. There was music in the air, and the butterfly kept time to it. The music must have been in my head, not real. But it was real enough. The hairs on the back of my neck twitched, and goose pimples rose on my forearms. Music filled the waterfall's auditorium and came to me over the roar of the water. My heart raced.

A voice shouted out, "Sorry if I scared you."

Standing up on the bank not more than five yards away was a tall lad with a flute. Seeing him, I realized there was an explanation for what had just happened. He was dressed in corduroy trousers and a sleeveless leather jacket, the normal attire of a farmworker. His mass of curly light brown hair came down to just above his shoulders. It was striking, considering short hair, back and sides, was the normal haircut of the day. He wore a big smile, and I instantly warmed to him.

He gave me a hand up the bank, and we walked down the path, away from the waterfall. Then we climbed a slope to a clearing, still in sight of the river but away from the waterfall's roar.

The lad's name was Llywelyn. He was seventeen, just coming up eighteen. He worked on his father's sheep farm two miles farther up the valley on the slopes of the Black Mountains. He'd never been out of Wales and wanted to know about London.

I gave a good description of Buckingham Palace and the Tower of London, but I disappointed him when he asked about Covent Garden because I knew nothing about the opera house, only the fruit and vegetable market. The bombing appalled him, so we didn't dwell on the subject.

He wanted to travel, play music, sing, and write poetry. It was fascinating to hear him talk about his dreams and plans. I'd never met anybody quite like him, not anyone who talked to me the way he did.

I told him I was going to be a farmer when I got older, but Llywelyn was sure I'd be something more creative. When he showed me his flute, I requested more music. He stood on the flat rock in the sunshine and played. I clapped enthusiastically at the end. Llywelyn appreciated his audience of one and asked me if I wanted more.

"Yes. Yes," I said.

"Then shout, encore, encore!" he directed.

I called out, "Encore, encore!" and he played more sweet music, followed by my spirited applause. Finally, he put down his flute. He stood silently before putting out his arms and breaking into song. He sang Welsh ballads, in Welsh. I clapped at the end of each song, shouting, "Encore, encore!" I didn't want him to stop.

Eventually, the show had to end. It was time to go. We set off up the path to a road that Llywelyn said would lead me directly into Talgarth more quickly than following the river. On the way up through the trees, he told me he often visited the waterfall and liked to practice there. Being there gave him inspiration. There was something special about the place. I wasn't the only one to feel it.

"The butterfly is often there, sometimes two of them," he said. "At times, I feel they perform for me. I've played some of my own compositions, and the butterflies danced to show their approval."

He said his mother was a music teacher. She'd taught him to play several instruments, including the piano, but the flute was his favourite. Eighteen months back, he'd won a scholarship to the Royal School of Music in London; but with the war, he was needed on the farm. However, his father had been promised two land-army girls who were supposed to arrive soon. They were trained for land and farming duties. Llywelyn had applied to the Royal Marines's music corps. Besides being trained to fight, they also gave concerts, many of them at the front line. "It boosts morale," he said. "I'm just waiting for my papers."

I wished him luck as we parted. "Need a haircut," I said.

"Be worth it just to be able to play and sing," he replied.

I returned to the waterfall several times during the next few months, but Llywelyn never appeared. Neither did the butterfly.

I arrived at Mrs. Davies's in the early evening, full of my discovery and the day's encounters. She knew of Llywelyn. His mother had given her children music lessons when they were younger. "A fine boy," she said. "Sad that one with so much talent has to go into the army. Suppose we all have to make sacrifices in these hard times. Anyhow, I'm sure his playing and singing will delight the troops."

Mrs. Davies had news for me. My father was coming to see me Thursday week and would stay for a few days. It had been quite a day, and what news to end it.

The days leading up to my father's arrival didn't pass quickly enough for me. School finished at the end of the following week, which was just as well, as I was getting into trouble for not paying attention. My appetite vanished, much to Mrs. Davies's annoyance. Finally, Thursday arrived. It was going to be a hot June day.

Dad was supposed to arrive at twelve o'clock. Mrs. Davies dressed me in a short-sleeved shirt, my best short trousers, socks, and clean, shiny black shoes. "There," she said. "Show your father you are well looked after. Now you keep clean, mind you."

With that, I went to the station platform half an hour early. Twelve o'clock passed. One o'clock passed. Still no train. Finally, a train arrived, but only three people got off, and my father wasn't one of them.

The stationmaster told me trains were running late, how late he couldn't say. There was a problem with connections at Bristol. He expected another train in an hour, but it might be delayed too. "Large troop movements going on," he said. "They have priority." He suggested I go have lunch, and he would keep an eye out for my father, but I wasn't hungry.

Instead, I walked down the path leading to the riverbank and helped myself to plums hanging on a branch over a hedge. The plums were still green, but I bit into two before deciding they were inedible.

I sat on the path and looked at the inviting river. Without thinking about the consequences, I tore off my shoes, socks, and shirt and into the river I went. I waded up and down, cupping my hands and taking a drink. I found catfish and poked them with my fingers to make them swim. All the time, I listened for the sound of a train.

It had to happen. It did. My foot slipped on a flat weed-covered slab. Feet in the air. Me in the river. One pair of soaked trousers. I figured I was in trouble with a capital T.

I scrambled up the bank, picked up my clothes, and worked my way through a hole in the hedge into the station garden with the plum trees. I took off my trousers, wrung them out, and hung them over a tree bough to dry in the sun. Fortunately, a hedge totally enclosed the station garden, so no one could see me.

An area of the garden was planted with bean, cabbages, and potatoes; and there was a clump of gooseberries and black currant bushes. I helped myself to some half-ripe black currants and tried a few gooseberries, but they needed several more weeks of sun to ripen.

Within half an hour, my trousers were only damp. Another fifteen minutes and they would be dry enough to put on.

That's when I heard the train, the unmistakable noise of a steam engine coming in. On went my damp trousers. I grabbed my shoes and socks and ran to the station platform.

A train had arrived. Toward the end of the platform, a soldier stood with his kit bag and rifle over his shoulder. It was my father. I dropped my shoes and socks and started running down the platform.

When he saw me, he dropped his kit bag and knelt to receive me in his arms. He picked me up, held me in the air and then put me down, and gave me another hug. "My, my! You are heavy," he said. "You've grown. What are they feeding you down here?"

We looked at each other, laughing and smiling. I was brown but not as brown as Dad. His face was almost the colour of dark brown shoes.

"Been taking in a bit of sun," he said. "It's wearing off now. Not a place I'd recommend for a holiday." He stood me back a pace and took a long look at me. "What on earth have you been up to?" He laughed.

I realized I wasn't dressed as Mrs. Davies had intended and told him what happened.

"The main thing is you're all right," he said. "I can see you're well looked after. Come on, show me where you live." He helped me put on my shoes and socks, took me by the hand, and we set off for Mrs. Davies's.

I skipped alongside, keeping in step with his long stride, chattering away at ten to the dozen. By the time we got to Mrs. Davies's, Dad had a potted history of my life since we'd last been together.

He didn't say what he'd been doing except to say that Mother was better now, almost fully recovered. He'd heard my sister was doing well. We'd go see her together. He hoped we might be able to return home by the end of the summer.

Mrs. Davies was pleased to see Dad. To welcome him, she had laid out a fine table with china plates and teacups I hadn't seen before. To me she said, "You need a whipping."

Dad thought a firing squad more appropriate. Anyhow, they both decided to put off my punishment for going into the water until the war ended, in case more able-bodied men were needed.

"God forbid," said Dad.

After I'd washed and changed, I joined Dad at the table. It felt like a dinner party. Midevening Owen made one of his rare visits to Mrs. Davies's with a bottle of dandelion wine in hand. They mostly talked about the war, and I was sent off to bed.

Mrs. Davies hoped her husband and son and her eldest daughter were coming for the weekend—their visits depended on transport—and if they came, they needed the other bedroom; so Dad was to share my large double bed with me, which was fine by him.

Dad didn't disturb me when he got in bed, but I woke in the night with a stomachache. At least, I thought I was awake. I was conscious of my stomachache and went off to the bathroom in a drowsy fog, the stomachache increasing. It was the unripe fruit having its revenge. After I relieved myself, I felt much better and returned to bed.

Suddenly, I sat bolt upright in bed, wide-awake. I hadn't been to the bathroom. It was a dream—no, worse, a nightmare. I'd crapped in my pyjamas. It had been years since anything like that happened to me. "Dad!" I cried out.

He woke immediately, saying something about not needing to tell him because the smell was bad enough. Pulling the bedclothes back, Dad got me to hold my pyjamas tight to my legs. He grabbed me under my armpits and knees and carried me into bathroom, where he stood me in the bathtub. He stripped off my pyjamas and gave me a sponge and soap to clean myself.

"Never good at this sort of thing," he muttered. "Would sooner have a tooth out than change your nappies. My god, you still stink as much." He went off to find me clean pyjamas.

I heard him talking to Mrs. Davies on the landing. They laughed—why, I didn't know as I didn't feel like laughing. I felt ashamed of myself. I figured what happened was my punishment for falling in the river.

Dad brought me clean pyjamas. I'd put my wet ones on the end of the tub and rinsed out the tub. He helped me with my pyjama top. I told him I was sorry and explained about the fruit.

"It's just one of those things that happen now and again," he said. "But not too often, I hope." He put me at ease. "Listen, where I've been, grown men do that in broad daylight, standing up—either because they can't move or because they're so frightened. I've had a few close shaves myself once or twice. Honest, been nearly scared shitless at times." With that, the subject was closed. We went back to bed with clean sheets and slept soundly until the next morning. What a way to welcome one's dad!

Dad spent the next day with me. In the morning, we visited the village, and then Owen showed Dad around the farmyard. He got on well with Dad. They sat on hay bales, talking together while I helped in the dairy.

In the afternoon, Dad joined me on the riverbank. He was happy just to sit in the sun and watch me play in the river. It must have been inviting because eventually he took off his shoes and socks and splashed around with me, shifting the bigger stones and poking the catfish.

Once I stood back and watched him. He seemed preoccupied, yet relaxed. Then we sat on the riverbank, allowing our feet to dry off in the sun. Dad brought up my school report. I'd given it to Mrs. Davies without opening it, and I was surprised to learn I wasn't doing well at school. I went, didn't I? I was seldom in trouble. Mrs. Davies and I usually got the homework done.

Dad said I was bright and was no trouble in class, but I was inclined to daydream. When I put in an effort, my work was good, but I was easily distracted. I kept quiet while he spoke. There was no point arguing. I did have trouble paying attention. My mind did wander. School never seemed real, but more of a pretend place. I wondered what sort of report Owen might have given me. The farm felt like real life.

Dad must have read my mind. "Owen says you're a fine boy. You're coping well under the circumstances."

Good old Owen, I thought. His opinion meant a lot to me.

"Once you get settled down, you'll be fine," Dad said. "In the meantime, try to concentrate a bit more on your studies. It's important, you know."

The importance of sitting in a classroom all day when I preferred to be outside escaped me, but after I promised to try to do better, Dad left it there.

We talked about my going back home in a month if things stayed as they were. Some children had already returned to their homes, but Dad said he was going to leave it to Mum to decide if and when.

Questions tumbled out of me. What did he mean for Mum to decide? Where was he going? Where had he been? What was the nasty gash on his left side?

I expected the usual curt replies to my war questions, his "It's not something to bother your head about." Instead, I got answers.

Perhaps he believed it could have been our last few days together because his attitude changed. He took me into his confidence. "I'll tell you, John. It's been hell just staying alive." He paused before adding, "And keeping others alive." He pointed to the sergeants' stripes on his rolled-up sleeve. "Last year, we were in Calais, France, as the worst hit the town. We had orders to hold out, but it was impossible. I got out a day before the Germans overran the place. I lost a lot of good men there. I arrived in England in time for the blitz and then spent three months in training at Aldershot. After a bit of leave, when I saw you last, I was shipped off to North Africa even though there was a threat of invasion here. The French battalions we relied on changed sides, and it was our job to hold off the Italians to keep them from getting into Egypt and taking the Suez Canal."

I must have looked puzzled, for Dad picked up a nearby stick and drew a map of North Africa in the dry silt bed at the river's edge. He pointed out Libya, Egypt, and coastal towns. He gave me brief details of the thrust of the desert war action and talked about the battle at Tobruk. "Prisoners were taken everywhere—thousands of them," he said. "We shipped many back here to help on the farms and in the factories. They were happy to be out of the war, lucky buggers. The effort we made was only a holding operation. The Jerries have decided to join the Italians and French in North Africa. The German panzer and tank division are going to make an enormous difference. It could be tough going."

"What about the wound?" I pointed.

"Oh, that. I caught a shell fragment about the size of an acorn. It must have been traveling to get through my flak jacket. I tell you it fair creased me up for a few days. That was the reason they flew me back to England. It required a minor operation to dig it out. It's fine now. I've been back in training, putting new recruits through their paces."

"Are you going back?" I was almost afraid to ask.

"Yes, shortly. I understand we're going to be joined by the Americans. They're already supplying some much-needed armament. Their tanks are going to make a difference. Tanks are going to be the key to this particular part of the war. It's more or less a tank war in the desert with troops mopping up behind. At least, it's clean."

"Clean?"

"Clean as a war can be," Dad said. "In the main, it's troops against troops, tanks against tanks. There are relatively few civilians involved, unlike here and in Russia. It's bad enough with the bombing here, but the figures coming out of Russia suggest several million women and children have died in the conflict so far—with more to come. Poor bastards. It fair makes my blood boil."

I felt angry too.

Dad abruptly changed the subject. He was keen to see the waterfall and then to see my sister.

Owen had told Dad he'd try to help out with transport, and that evening, he showed up with an old army lorry that belonged to the Home Guard.

"A flanker," Dad said, smiling.

"A flanker?" I asked.

"A deal on the side," Dad said. "An army term for fiddling."

Owen said Dad could have the lorry for four days. Owen had filled the tank and produced two more filled five-gallon cans. When Dad said, "I can't thank you enough," Owen just grinned.

"Good old soldier," Dad said to me after Owen left.

"Soldier?"

"Yes. He volunteered at seventeen and served at the front in the last two years of the First World War. He's seen more action than I have and been decorated for bravery."

Owen had never said a word to me.

The next morning, we took off for Hay to pick up my sister. She cried and cried when she saw us, and the hugging went on for ten minutes. She showed Dad her room, the garden, and her Wendy house. We all ended up in the Wendy house, happy to be together.

For the next four days, we visited the Brecons, the Black Mountains, and the waterfall. We played in the garden, chattering away about what each of us had been doing. We talked about Mum, GranDad, our plans for after the war, and school. We didn't discuss the possibility of Dad not surviving the war. It passed through my mind, but I didn't say anything. Nothing was going to spoil our four days.

Our time with Dad ended too quickly. He and I returned from my sister's late at night. He got up early the next morning, dressed, and got ready to leave before he woke me. Neither of us knew what to say to each other. He picked up his kit bag, slung his rifle over his shoulder, and gave me a final wave, leaving me sitting up in bed.

Emptiness filled the room, and I felt colder. A voice inside my head, some sort of inner presence, told me Dad would be all right. As the minutes passed, the reassuring voice comforted me. I slipped out of bed, knelt as Mum had taught me, and prayed to God for Dad.

In Mother's latest letter, she said that the schools had been commandeered as billeting for prisoners of war and forces personnel. Although food and fuel were adequate, there was severe rationing. She thought we should stay where we were even though she missed us very much. My hopes to return to her at the summer's end were dashed.

Mother did come for Christmas. She stayed at my sister's, and I spent those days with her. Having no transport, Mother couldn't take us out, so we were confined to the house because of heavy rains. Although I was pleased to see her, I was anxious to return to my now-familiar surroundings, my Wellingtons, mackintosh, farmyard, and Owen. It felt strange, but Talgarth had become home to me.

Leading up to spring, I had a series of colds and sore throats. The diagnosis was tonsillitis. They had to come out. After the operation, my confinement, in case of infection, lasted six weeks. During that time, I became an avid reader of comics, adventure stories, and eventually books. When I finally returned to school in the early summer, I approached my schoolwork with a new interest. Reading had opened my mind, and for the first time, I actually became interested in school, books, and exercises. Working hard at home, I took pride in doing my homework myself.

The summer term was also most enjoyable for the playground activities. I'd been accepted as part of the school players and joined in playground games as they came in and out of season. Flicking cigarette cards, playing marbles and conkers had their weeks. I was particularly adept at playing five stones. We played soccer from one end of the playground to the other when a boy brought a prized used tennis ball to school. An owner of a tennis ball was a popular lad. For cricket, we used stumps chalked on the school wall.

My favorite team game was Knock Down Ginger, frowned on by playground attendants. The game was fun but not for the timid. We'd team up in fours. One boy bent down from the waist and put his head and hands against the school wall. The second, third, and fourth boys followed suit behind, placing their heads between the legs of boy in front and grasping their legs firmly with both hands. Our backs formed a bridge or platform for the rest of the boys to take a running jump and leapfrog as far up the backs of the bridge as they could. One by one, the pile on the boys' backs got longer and higher. The winning team was the one to take the most leapfroggers before collapsing or shaking off a leapfrogger. Teamwork was vital for success. The team needed a strong middle, a good anchor, and a solid tail man. Planning was the key to winning. Long and high leapfroggers tried to expose a weak link, and that was the critical part of the game. Individual weights meant little. A large, fat boy was useless if he couldn't leapfrog over the tail end. Once we felt any instability of the pile on our backs, we'd begin a rhythmic heaving and lurching, trying to shake off a leapfrogger.

The leapfroggers countered with a rhythmic bouncing. Invariably, everyone ended up in a heap of arms and legs with much arguing as to who gave way first, an expected end to a competitive game.

Just before the summer term ended, Owen met me at the school gate. The look on his face told me something was seriously wrong. He wasted no time giving me the bad news.

Mrs. Davies's oldest son's plane had gone down into the North Sea, exploding before impact. A daylight search revealed no survivors. He was posted as missing, believed to be dead. "There is little hope," Owen told me. "There's nothing anyone can say to Mrs. Davies to give her hope. We pray they'll find his body, so he can have a decent burial. But it's unlikely. The North Sea is a treacherous place, and there's too much going on for anyone to spend time searching for bodies." Owen paused. "He was a fine boy. Such a waste." His voice choked.

We walked in silence. My own thoughts were mixed. I thought, What if that had been my dad, my mother, or granddad. Will I lose Dad one day? How will I feel? These thoughts had often entered my head. They were hard to suppress. The worries that plagued me swelled to the surface, along with grief for Mrs. Davies. I felt insecure and frightened. The wall I'd built around myself, shutting out negative thoughts, crumbled. As suppressed fears became a reality, I wanted to cry, but tears wouldn't come.

I focused on Mrs. Davies. She hadn't said much about the war, her family's involvement, or her fears. She kept her thoughts to herself. Whenever one of her family turned up, she was excited and came out of her shell. They were a close-knit family the war had driven apart.

Owen interrupted my thoughts. "She got the news just after you left for school this morning." He said the doctor had been to see her, and her husband and other son were due back home. "They will possibly be there by now," he said. "Under the circumstances, it's best if you come to stay with me and leave Mrs. Davies and her family to themselves."

When we got to the house, I saw bunches of flowers with attached notes all along the wall by the side of the gate. Obviously, the bad news had already reached her village friends. I told Owen I wanted to get some flowers. He pointed to a bunch of white roses, just coming out of bud. The card was signed "John."

"Did that for you," he said.

I wanted to take them inside and give them to Mrs. Davies, but Owen told me to leave them where they were. "It's the right thing to do," he assured me. "Mrs. Davies will see the flowers all in good time. Just at the moment wouldn't be the right time."

We went into the kitchen by the side door. Mr. Davies, his son, and the doctor were there. Mrs. Davies sat in a chair by the side of the range. I ran across the kitchen and threw my arms around her neck. She buried her head in my shoulder and gave me a tight hug. Tears welled in my eyes.

I kept repeating, "I'm sorry, I'm sorry."

Gradually her grip relaxed, and I felt Owen lifting me away. He helped me pack GranDad's suitcase, and we left by the front door.

I stayed with Owen for a few weeks. Mrs. Davies left home to stay with her husband in Port Talbot. She came to see me before she left, looking very tired. Her eyes had lost their sparkle. Her hair was going grey. She wished me and my family well.

Another episode of my life closed.

During the weeks with Owen, he and Mother exchanged letters. After reading one of her letters, he told me I was to return home. He made arrangements for my departure. I felt mixed emotions. I had learnt so much in the nearly two years away and had long since felt comfortable with my adopted surroundings. The abrupt ending of my evacuation and the circumstances clouded the excitement I should have felt in returning home.

Owen saw me off at the station early one morning. The weather was fitting—dull and overcast with a light drizzle. Our parting initially lacked emotion. I didn't know what to say, and Owen was reserved as usual. He was more concerned over my understanding his travel instructions. "Can't lose you now," he said. "Your dad would never forgive me."

With his customary efficiency, he'd packed me off with a larger suitcase than I'd come with. I had a satchel full of sandwiches and a bottle of lemonade. He'd written down each station where I was to change trains on a postcard.

Standing in the train compartment, I got Owen's last-minute instructions. I promised to work hard at school and to write to tell him how I was getting on. The train steamed up and lurched, ready to pull out of the station. The guard's whistle blew, warning people to stand clear of the train. Owen put his hand out, intending for me to shake it as a final good-bye. Instead, I threw my arms around his neck, holding on until the train's motion pulled me off. Owen's eyes glistened. A tear ran down my cheek. I waved furiously until Owen and the station were out of sight.

Chapter 7

SURPRISES

The train journey went as Owen planned, with changes at Bristol and London. The results of the Luftwaffe bombing were a chilling sight. Bristol looked like a Lilliputian town visited by a drunken giant armed with a flamethrower leaving a trail of flattened and gutted buildings in its wake.

As the train moved into and out of London, the scene was one of greater devastation. Area after area, mile after mile, pockmarks of destruction littered the landscape. Areas of rubble, twisted metal, and bombed-out buildings were larger than some of the smaller towns I'd passed on the train. In one older London section, I saw that the tarred wooden blocks used for centuries to pave the narrow roadways were embers.

All across London's skyline were flotillas of barrage balloons. Pillboxes, with their ominous gun slits and antiaircraft gun emplacements, had grown up in many of the bombsites. Looking down into the streets, I saw the bustle of camouflaged lorries. Some carried solders, some supplies, and some piled high with crates of potatoes, cabbages, and root crops. A few carried coal, hay, or straw. I saw horse-drawn carts in most streets. Alongside the railway embankment, waited row after row of open railway trucks, all containing coal. Armed soldiers guarded the coal to keep people from pinching it.

Alongside the railway track, groups of men worked on repairs. Most dressed in normal clothes with large bright-coloured patches sewn into holes cut into their trousers and jackets. They were Italian prisoners of war. One or two armed men from the Home Guard accompanied each group of twenty or thirty prisoners.

Mother and Chalky greeted me at Epsom and made a great fuss over me. They couldn't get over how much I'd grown. Mother looked older, but fit and well. Chalky had hardly changed.

There was no transport available. Buses weren't running, and there were no taxis. Petrol was rationed.

Chalky said, "It's shank's pony. We're walking."

Mother brought the pram with her. We tied my case to the top. It was a good hour's walk out of town to home. We chattered all the way.

I learned three pieces of good news. First, GranDad was fine. Mother saw him recently. He was, as GranDad put it, "shacked up in a hotel for the time being. It's a bit crowded but comfortable."

Dad was surviving the North African campaign. Mother had gotten letters from him. He sunned himself somewhere along the Mediterranean after capturing German tanks. He was part owner of the biggest scrap yard in the world. He complained of the flies and the heat and had palled up with some Americans. For the first time in three years, he enjoyed good food and beer.

Chalky's news was great. After a year or more of uncertainty and fear, he learned through the Red Cross that his son was a prisoner of war. He had spent time in a camp hospital with a minor injury but had fully recovered. That's all Chalky knew, but after fearing the worst, his son being a prisoner of war was good news. Chalky had managed to get down to Brighton to see his grandchildren. The last time, by twisting a few arms and calling in favours, he delivered the rocking horse.

At each intersection, we passed a pillbox. Pillboxes blocked all but the narrowest of access into the town with long canal-like tank traps. Bomb craters dotted the roads. Mother had lost her rear windows twice. On the other side of the estate, three houses had been severely damaged by a bomb at the rear end of their gardens. At the entrance to the estate, a large public family air-raid shelter had been built. Most surprising to me was the huge areas of common land and woods that had been cultivated. There were rows of potatoes and other root crops and corn. Interspersed throughout the fields were islands forty or fifty yards across of original woodland. Chalky believed they had been left so that we didn't lose our wildlife completely. I figured they'd also make good hiding places for tanks.

On entering the estate, I saw shops on the left-hand side with all their windows boarded up. Mother said the shops lost them three times, and they'd been waiting months for replacements.

"May as well leave them boarded up," she said. "They have nothing to sell. Everything is rationed. They only open for a few hours each week, except for the shoe repairer. He's always busy." Mother pointed at her well-worn shoes. "Had these nearly three years, and they've been resoled four or five times. Oh, to be able to go out and buy a new pair of shoes. What a luxury!"

Mother said most things had been in short supply and severely rationed. Goods were gradually becoming available, although there were queues for everything. She and Chalky hadn't seen beef for over eighteen months.

Mother said, "If I'm lucky and happen to be at the shop at the right time, I can get fish, whale, or horse meat."

"Eaten our dogs ages ago," joked Chalky although at one time, it might have come to that in the larger towns. "Rabbits are scarcer. Everybody's out snaring them."

Chalky still had his rabbits and kept a few pigs on his allotment at the rear of the garden. "Getting food for them is a problem," he said. "The ministry men help out. Should do too. They take the pigs off me. I'm not allowed to own my own. But they can't count." He winked at Mother. "The odd pig escapes the ministry eye."

Mother kept ducks for their eggs, but keeping foxes out of the cages was a problem. Foxes killed two ducks only a few weeks before. Mother buried them, but Chalky dug them up again and cooked them.

Such were the tales I heard as we walked home.

Chalky had a surprise for me, but he wouldn't tell me what it was. I'd have to wait until tomorrow.

At home, I met the nurse staying with Mother—the other nurse had left a few weeks ago to fill an overseas position—and was smitten at first sight. She was Irish, twenty-one or twenty-two, slim but well proportioned with wavy dark auburn hair hanging down to her shoulder blades and bright green eyes. Her face lit up when she smiled, revealing a beautiful set of teeth. She wore little makeup, and her complexion reminded me of ladies in soap advertisements I'd seen at train stations. Her name was Christine. She said I could call her Chris.

Christine liked me. She told Mum she was going to wait until I grew up. Mum told her not to be so saucy. "He's just a young pup. He doesn't know what you are on about. Don't tease him."

Mum was wrong. I knew what she was on about. Young as I was, nature was at work. Something stirred inside me. Roll on, growing up, I thought. Love had touched me.

I was to have my downstairs bedroom back. Christine slept upstairs in the rear bedroom, my sister's room. Mum slept in the front bedroom as usual.

My sister was happy where she was and wouldn't be coming back yet. Besides attending a private school, she had music and ballet lessons. Mum was confident she was in the best place, at least for a while.

"Nothing around here for her," she said. "The reason I had you come home was that I didn't feel it good for you to move another time. Owen appeared to be fine, but he lived on his own and worked long hours on the farm. He was a widower. His grown-up children were away from home." Mother knew more than I did. "Poor Mrs. Davies," she added. "You must write her tomorrow."

Before Mother prepared supper, she put my pyjamas on the clotheshorse in front of the fire and told me to take a bath. She'd already run the water for me.

I was sitting in the bath, just about finished, when the door opened.

"Don't mind me, do you?" Chris said. "Must wash. I'm late for night shift. I have to wipe my face and clean my teeth." She stood against the washbasin, dressed in a thin white three-quarter-length slip covering her kickers. She didn't seem to have anything on underneath. If she did, it wasn't holding much in place. Everything moved side to side as she washed.

I knew it was rude to stare, but I stared, enjoying the view.

She turned to pick up a face towel and gave me a smile.

I slapped the flannel over my privates—it had shot bolt upright—and pretended to look for the soap.

Chris dipped her hand in the bathwater and found it. She picked up the flannel and asked if I wanted her to do my back.

I felt my face go bright red and worried I might explode.

Just in time, Mother poked her head inside the door. She had my pyjamas. Seeing Chris, she told her not to walk around like that because I was getting to be a big boy now. Chris put down the flannel and soap, flashed me a smile, and left the bathroom.

I dressed quickly and joined Mother in the dining room for supper, pretending nothing had happened and that I was calm.

Chalky's surprise for me was a two-wheeled bicycle, a replica of his, newly painted, black, and shiny. It had been his son's. He'd had trouble getting decent secondhand tyres. "Like gold dust," he said. "The inner tubes have patches on, but they should last a while." The brake block he'd made from segments cut from an old lorry tyre.

He lowered the saddle as far as it would go, so I could reach the pedals, but I'd grown more than he anticipated and reached them easily. I don't know who was more excited, Chalky or me. After a few false starts—with Chalky steadying the bicycle for me—I mastered the knack of riding.

Chalky got out his bicycle, and we rode up and down the road. He put me through a series of exercises—stopping, starting, signaling, turning left, turning right—and reported back to Mother that I was competent enough to ride on my own.

For the next weeks, I practically lived on the bicycle, exploring around the estate and surroundings. I followed the grass tracks across the cultivated fields and along the dirt tracks in the woods, where I found bomb craters, some forty feet wide and twenty feet deep. I came across the remains of three German planes, all badly broken up and ransacked for anything useful. From pictures I'd seen, I recognized one as a Junker 88. Wedged down behind a broken seat, I found a leather belt with a sheath and dagger attached to it. The double-edged dagger had a blade seven inches long with a brass top on a leather-bound handle. The brass had an embossed Nazi swastika. The leather belt had a large brass eagle fashioned into a buckle. The belt was on the large side for me, so I dug another hole with the dagger and wore it home, much to my mother's horror.

She confiscated the belt and dagger from me and told me to put them in the middle drawer of the clothes chest in her bedroom. When I opened the wrong drawer, I discovered a pistol lying on top of clothes. Just as I picked it up to examine it, Mother came into the room with freshly ironed clothes. She told me to put the pistol down and never touch it again. "It's loaded," she said. "The safety catch is on, but it's very dangerous to play with guns." She made me promise never to touch it.

I wanted to know why she had it.

After promising to keep it a secret, she told me Father had given it to her early on in the war when he first came back from France. It was a German Luger he had taken off a dead soldier.

"Dad took me over into the woods and taught me how to use it," she said. "He was worried about a possible invasion. He told me to take out as many Jerries as I could and then . . . ," she stopped.

"And then?" I asked.

"You don't want to know the rest," she said. "Go on downstairs. Your tea is ready."

I was sure I knew what Mother was going to say. She was to turn the pistol on herself and maybe on me before that. I didn't ask more questions about the pistol, but the thought haunted me for some time: my mother might kill me.

I played out the possible incident in my mind for weeks. At first, I was upset with my thoughts and the possibilities. Eventually, I worked out how I could protect my mother if the worst happened. I planned to hide out in the woods and trap rabbits for food. Somehow, we would survive. I'd see to it.

Getting around on the bicycle, I met and palled up with another boy who had returned from evacuation. His name was Ronnie. He was nine months older and about my size. He became my best friend but not without a fistfight. He wanted to ride my bicycle, but I wouldn't let him. He punched me. I punched him back. We ended up wrestling on the ground, trading blows, the bicycle on top of us. I was about to bite his ear when two passing ladies broke up the fight. They knew our mothers and gave us a good ticking off. One suggested I might let Ronnie have a ride on the bike. After all, he had no father and little else. I reluctantly agreed.

"You're some scrapper," Ronnie said, smiling. "Thought I could beat anybody my size. It'd be best if we were friends." He held out his hand, and I shook it.

We took turns riding down the hill from the top of the estate around the sharp bend into the road where I lived. We gathered speed until we reached the bottom of the crescent. I'd ride on the crossbar while he pedaled, and then we'd change places. We managed to get up some speed, leaning over at a perilous angle as we rounded the bend. We had a few wobbles but stayed on the bike.

Midafternoon, two older boys turned up with a homemade trolley made of a builder's plank with pram wheels on either end. The driver steered it by pulling on a short length of looped washing line. The line fastened to either side of the front axle, nailed onto a piece of wood, pivoted at the centre by a through bolt.

The plank was just about long enough for all four of us to sit on. Ronnie and I rode as passengers. Twenty miles an hour might not seem fast, but crouched down on that trolley, we could have been heading for the sound barrier; such was the feeling of speed.

If more boys turned up in the afternoon, we'd play cricket. The pitch was the centre of the road. The wicket was the smaller of the pig bins placed on the corner of the crescent. We fashioned a bat from a fence piece. We used a tennis ball or sometimes a hard sorbo rubber ball. The rules were simple.

The bowler bowled off twenty-two paces. The batsman hit the ball and ran to the bowler's end for a run. If the ball hit the pig bin or a fielder caught it in midair, the batsman was out. The batsman was also out if he hit the ball over the hedges into one of the adjacent gardens, but he got six runs as compensation. "Six and out!" we'd cry.

I soon learnt to protect my wicket with the bat and only hit off-line balls, scurrying well and staying in for quite a while.

"Stubborn sod," Ronnie said at times, trying to bowl me out.

We were all going to play cricket for England one day. Making the England team was the pinnacle of sporting achievement.

Toward summer's end, Ronnie and I decided to explore the back of my garden. Mum was out at her day job, and Chris was upstairs asleep. We climbed over the chestnut fencing, walked across the allotments, and pushed our way through a gap in the bamboo hedge. We stood in an orchard of apple and pear trees. Beyond the rows of fruit trees, the ground sloped down to a huge expanse of lawn. Tall trees edged the lawn on two sides. Rhododendron and azalea bushes interspersed with lilac trees lined the other sides.

An enormous greenhouse ran the length of the rectangle to the right-hand side of the orchard. It was filled with grapevines, black grapes at one end and white grapes at the other. Rows of tomato plants covered with ripe tomatoes hid underneath the grapevines. We also found patches of cucumbers and rows of lettuce in various growth stages. Using old brown paper fertilizer bags, neatly stacked in a corner, Ronnie and I gathered what we'd found, one bag for his mother and one for mine. Before leaving, we picked up two more bags because we decided to pick apples.

"Too good to miss," Ronnie said. He gave a bunk up to the first branch.

I climbed up through the tree, picked off the choice apples, and threw them down to Ronnie. With the sacks half full, we decided we had enough. I was nearly at the top. Ronnie took the sacks out through the gap in the bamboo hedge and was coming back for the last sack when he shouted that someone was coming. He grabbed the last sack and disappeared through the hedge.

I peered out through the branches. A man walked toward the trees. He had bright coloured patches sewn to his clothes. Shit, I thought, a prisoner of war. I was too high, and he was too close for me to climb down and sneak away. I figured if I froze, he might not see me, but he did.

He waved his arms at me and beckoned me to come down.

"Not on your life," I shouted. "Come up and get me."

When he came closer, I picked off apples and threw them at him. I missed, but he took a few paces back. He stood, looking up at me, while I stared at him. After pulling a wallet from his jacket pocket, he took out a postcard, pointed at it, and shouted at me, gesticulating with his hands. His English was barely understandable, but understanding his body language was easier. He said he was a friend and that he too had a family.

I had a lot of preconceived distrust built up regarding prisoners of war. "Clear off!" I shouted and threw another apple at him.

He pointed to himself and called, "Friend!"

I waved him over to the tree base and pointed to the postcard, signaling he should leave it there. I waved my arms and told him to go away. He understood, put his postcard where I'd pointed, and walked back halfway across the lawn. I climbed down, keeping an eye on him on the while. Finally, I dropped from the lowest limb to the ground and picked up what I'd thought was a postcard, but it was a photograph.

He stayed where he was while I had a good look at it. In the photograph, he stood with his wife, son, and daughter—they were smartly dressed and smiling—in front of a large house with a garden full of flowers and fruit trees. "My family," he called. "My house. My garden. I am friend. I no harm. I—"

Ronnie burst through the hedge with Chalky.

"He's all right," Chalky called to me. "Name's Mario. Italian." As he grew closer, he continued, "Been with us for about a year. He's acting as gardener and caretaker at the big house up through the trees. They shut down the house two years ago. I believe it was a private school. The ministry took it over. I don't think they know what to do with it. Come on. I'll show you."

Chalky introduced us to Mario, and we set off to the far corner of the lawn. We made our way up through a wide grass pathway surrounded by rhododendrons that led into sloping gardens. There were flowers everywhere. Particularly striking were huge rose beds in shades of red, pink, yellow, and white.

The mansion house was large, at least twenty bedrooms. "Not sure when it was built," Chalky said. "Probably in Queen Victoria's time when it became fashionable for wealthy people to come here to drink and bathe in the water."

"What water?" I asked, looking around for a swimming pool.

"Water brought up from wells. You, my lad, are living on Wells Estate, the home of health-giving Epsom salts. There are wells dotted around the grounds. There's one in the orchards. I believe there's another one in the mansion."

We had a quick tour of the mansion, which seemed to go on forever, and then left to return home. On the way back, Chalky said, "It's all right to come into these grounds, but you shouldn't take anything without Mario's permission. Otherwise, it's stealing. Not that you would get into trouble at the moment as we don't have a policeman around here. The nearest we have to the law is me, and I don't think I want to lock you up." Chalky laughed. "Most of the produce goes to the hospital."

Ronnie and I got the message. Mother was pleased with what I brought home. She suggested I make a friend of Mario if "this is what he's growing," so I did. I'd find him working somewhere on the estate and help him. Afterward, I came back home with a bag of something he'd grown. On several Sundays, Mother invited him to join Chalky, Chris—if she were home—and me for lunch. What we ate depended on what Chalky or Mario bartered for.

Mario enjoyed his Sunday lunch. So did Chalky as Mario always brought at least two large bottles of homemade wine. "Good wine," Mario said in halting English. "But I made better back in Italy. You must come after the war." We promised we would.

It seemed strange that Dad was fighting and capturing Italians and we were sitting down with one and enjoying his company. Possibly, he was one Dad or his comrades had captured as Mario had been in the desert campaign. He wouldn't talk about his war experiences though. If we brought it up, he screwed up his face and shook his head and said, "Bah, no good place."

Through the summer and into the winter, we felt and heard the heavy throbbing drone of bomber planes. I'd sit on the front garden wall and watch the planes pass. Wave after wave went by, flying in box formation. The noise continued well into the night, abating for a while and then in the early morning, starting up again. The morning noise was different from the evening noise. Splattering and missing engine firing was audible as damaged aircraft returned from a raid.

Chalky joined me on the wall and watched the planes with me. He pointed out various types. He also showed me planes flying up high above the formation. We barely made out Spitfire and Hurricane fighter escort planes, flying along as protection for the bombers.

Chalky raised his head to the sky and said, "Off to Germany, my lads. My heart goes with you. Good luck. Give the blighters some of their own medicine. See how they like it." Then he turned to me and said, "Some brave boys up there."

It felt good to know we were hitting back. Although I'd seen firsthand what happened in Bristol and London and pictures of Coventry, there was no pity in my heart for what was in store for the Germans. In my book, they deserved everything we threw at them.

Each day, the wireless informed us where the bombers had dropped their calling cards. Chalky had a European map on his study wall. He stuck coloured pins in it to mark cities as news came through. By the next summer, there were over one hundred pins, indicating major attacks on German cities. Hearing the drone of bombers overhead became a way of life right up until the war's end.

Often, hundreds of strips of thin silver metal foil fluttered down, carried by the wind. Chalky said, "It's a delightfully simple idea to foul up the German radar. A few planes can be made to look like five hundred bombers. The Germans have no idea until very late which directions the real bombers come from or where the targets were that night."

Occasionally, although more infrequently, the Germans hit back, and the air-raid sirens sounded off. I'd go under the stairs. Mother and Chris—when she was home—slept under the Morrison table. Mother had someone install a heavy, rigid steel frame that supported a sloping steel corrugated sheet that fitted under the line of the stairs.

"Belt and braces," she said. "I think the house could fall in, and you'd still be all right."

To ease the tension and pass time, Mother read aloud by torchlight. I'd listen from under the stairs with the door open. When Mother finished, she and Chris asked me to tell a story.

"Come on, John, tell us about the farm," Christine said. She loved my stories and got caught up in them.

When I told about the waterfall, I elaborated. "Swishing down. Pouring down. Water cascading everywhere." I stopped and then added, "Gurgle. Gurgle. Psss. Psss," to imitate the noise of a running tap and having some fun with Christine.

"John, you're a little sod!" Christine shouted.

Every evening and morning, we put up and took down the window blackout covers. It only took a few minutes. By then, the covers were fastened onto stout wooden frames that fitted over slips placed around the window frames. It was a vast improvement to being blacked out all day long.

Midautumn Chris came home agitated. She'd heard about a nurse who'd been attacked and assaulted when she took a shortcut through a churchyard. The woman had put up a fight, and her face was severely bruised. Because Chris was frightened to walk through the churchyard on her own, she had to walk a mile farther to the hospital. She'd been promised a bicycle ages ago, but it still hadn't arrived.

Mother decided I should walk Chris to work of an evening. Chalky found lights to put on my bicycle. He reminded me to turn them off if the air-raid siren sounded. Just before we set off on the first evening, I asked Mother if I could wear the belt and dagger I'd found in the German aeroplane. I considered asking for the pistol, but I knew better. Mother hesitated, but encouraged by Christine, she relented and allowed me to wear the belt and dagger. It made me feel brave even though I had no idea what to do with dagger.

I had helped kill rabbits, I'd seen pigs slaughtered, and I could wring a chicken's neck; so I was certain I could stick a knife into someone, or at least try. I think Mother had inkling what I was capable of, and that was why she didn't allow me to wear the dagger out for play. If I got into a fight, I might lose my head and use it. She was wise.

Christine and I started off just after dusk. Thick clouds swirled overhead, plunging us in and out of darkness. I walked alongside Christine, pushing my bicycle until we reached the top of the estate. Then I rode alongside her until we came to the asphalt path running downhill across the common. She had a job keeping up with me. "Slow down," she ordered. "I don't intend to run to work."

At a walking pace, the bicycle was unstable, so I got off and walked beside her.

Christine said, "I've got a brilliant idea, well worth a try." She took her nurse's cape off and put if over the handlebars. She pulled her uniform skirt up to her thighs. "It's too dark for anyone to see me." She put her leg over the crossbar and sat on the saddle with her feet on the ground.

In the moonlight, I glimpsed my first view of black stocking tops, suspenders, and white thighs.

Christine told me to sit on the handlebars and hold on tight. Using her feet for propulsion and braking, she scooted down the footpath, gaining speed all the time, whooping and shrieking with laughter. When we hit an unexpected bump where the asphalt path met a roadway, the jolt nearly threw us off, and the bicycle weaved side to side down the roadway. Christine managed to stop it at a gravel track turning off to the left, the rear pathway across the common to the church. We dismounted.

Gorse bushes, decaying bracken, hawthorn bushes, and the silhouette of silver birch trees flanked the gravel path on either side. We walked about one hundred yards when we came to the rear entrance of the church. The gate suspended between two large stone pillars and creaked from lack of oiling. Tall dark yew trees surrounded the churchyard. A slight wind sprang up and caused the trees' shadows to move over the large tomb and memorial flagstones lining the graves.

The whole place gave me the creeps. Goose pimples rose on my arms. The moonlight and shadows played trick with my eyes. I thought I saw movement near the graves. Our feet scrunched on the gravel path. An owl hooted, spooking up my adrenaline.

Christine started up a lighthearted conversation as we walked around to the front of the church. I had the dagger in my right hand as I controlled the bicycle with my left. Suddenly, we both stopped. I froze. The bicycle fell over.

Walking toward us across the front church lawn was the unmistakable figure of a man. He carried on walking toward us, making no noise over the grass.

"Good evening," he called from about fifteen yards.

"Good evening," we both replied, my voice high-pitched, and the dagger clenched in my fist.

As he got closer, we saw he was Home Guard soldier, complete with rifle. "Everything all right, miss?" he asked.

"It is now," she said. "You fair gave me a start."

"Sorry about that," he said. "I have orders to look in at the churchyard two or three times an evening. You heard about what happened? Terrible business."

"Yes," Christine said. "I have my bodyguard with me." She nodded at me.

"Good idea." The officer eyed my dagger.

After exchanging pleasantries, Christine and I walked out onto the roadway at the front of the church. I'd already decided to return by road, the long way around.

Christine thanked me for escorting her and pointed up the road to the hospital entrance and said, "I'm sure I'll be safe now. Only a few minutes' walk."

I left and cycled back home, the long way around.

Christine's bicycle didn't come for another six weeks. When she was on duty, either I or Chalky—if he wasn't working—carried on with the escort service. As far as I knew, there were no further incidents at the churchyard.

Harvesting the potato fields started in late October. The potato tops were already turning brown and dying back, but the harvest had been delayed due to a labour shortage. People threatened to help themselves if the crop were left much longer as there was a severe shortage with strict rationing. Notices warning of penalties had been posted around the fields, warning of consequences to anyone caught pilfering.

Finally, three potato-lifting machines arrived along with thirty land-army girls and eighty Italian prisoners of war. A makeshift tent appeared amongst the bracken on the common. Once the harvesting started, it was all bustle.

Mother saw a notice in a shopwindows asking for help picking and sacking potatoes and volunteered me. She said it would keep me out of mischief, and I'd earn pocket money. I got six pennies a day working from dawn until dusk. As a bonus, I got a sack of thirty pounds of potatoes each Friday for the three weeks I worked. These, plus the six or seven I sneaked inside my shirt every evening before leaving the fields, provided Mother with one hundred fifty pounds of potatoes.

"With the ration allowance, we'll have enough to see us through the winter," she said.

When Mother decided to visit my sister for three weeks, she made arrangements with Christine and Chalky to look after me. I had to stay at Chalky's the nights Christine was on duty. Chalky had made a wooden dollhouse, about the size of two shoeboxes, for my sister. It opened at the front and showed four rooms of tiny furniture. He even wallpapered the walls. Mother took it with her.

Christine often teased me, squaring up to me in a boxing fashion if she thought I was getting out of line. Her cooking was not Mum's. It was awful, so I preferred to eat at Chalky's. If I got hungry, I'd dip into Mum's preserved fruit and jam jars from the pantry. "When the worms got to my stomach," as Christine put it, I prepared odd snacks. The most bizarre meal I made myself was two stale bread slices with margarine layered with preserved rhubarb and topped with cream spooned off the milk.

Christine refused to try my concoction. "I'm sure it's fattening, besides it's revolting," she said.

Ronnie came around to play, especially on wet days. We enjoyed draughts. Christine taught us to play cards. She hated to lose. When we got the hang of the game, she either changed the rules or taught us another game. One day Ronnie and I decided to play a joke on her. We got a second pack of cards from the bridge box. When Christine dealt us our cards, we sneaked cards from our laps into our hands. However, our hands of four aces, four kings, or four queens were too much for Christine, especially when she was sitting with two queens herself. Her cries of "Cheats!" and playful clips around our ears finished our card games.

The Morrison table doubled as a table tennis table. Books served as a net and as bats. We made a ball of tightly compressed paper bound with cotton. Neither Ronnie nor I could beat Christine at this improvised form of table tennis. Her reactions were quick.

Early in the second week after Mum left, Chalky brought around a pair of stilts he'd made for me. He'd nailed wooden blocks onto a piece of two-by-one-inch timber. Ronnie and I had great fun learning to walk with them. Christine tried to master walking with them, but they were on the small side, so Chalky made her a pair too.

One afternoon Christine and I were out in the garden racing each other on the stilts when a clunk clunk clunk came down the pathway at the side of the house. There was Chalky on a pair of stilts. We spent the afternoon playing soccer on stilts, using a tin can as a ball.

The Sunday afternoon before Mother returned, Christine persuaded me to visit the hospital with her. It was her day off, but she wanted to go in as it was visitor's afternoon, and she knew some of her patients wouldn't receive visitors.

To convince me, she said, "I'd like to introduce this strapping young man I've found to some of my favorite patients," as she ruffled my hair. She was always pulling my leg.

The hospital was built in several acres of grounds. The entrance layout, through large gates, typical of pastoral manor houses, had a drive sweeping through the parkland with well-spaced matured oak, beech, and elm trees that lent a touch of elegance to the estate. The old manor house served as the administration centre.

After the First World War, taxes, and the recession of the 1930s, many such establishments fell into disrepair, and the state took them over. This particular estate had long since been a home for the mentally handicapped, including the criminally insane. Locals referred to it as the loony bin. It wasn't a place to end up in as few people ever left.

A sign directed us to the Forces Rehabilitation Centre, a cluster of buildings set on their own in rows of newly built Nissen huts, approximately forty feet long by twenty feet wide, constructed in half-round sheeted asbestos.

"Not exactly the Hilton," Christine said. "But we make do."

Asphalted pathways surrounded by lawns connected the buildings. Some men attended to flowerbeds while others stood in groups talking or sat in chairs or wheelchairs enjoying the late autumn sun. There were over a hundred men, with a sprinkling of nurses. There were few visitors, but Christine said we were half an hour early. Visiting time didn't start until two thirty. As we approached, Christine got waves, catcalls, and wolf whistles. She didn't appear bothered but just smiled and kept walking.

The patients were dressed in light blue suits. Several wore white scarves. I saw men with one or two legs missing. Those walking on crutches managed with one leg. They had folded back the other trouser leg to where the leg or foot had been severed or amputated. Men with only one arm had empty jacket sleeves hanging down by their sides. Some men had suffered burns. Their hands and face tissue was badly scarred.

I felt uncomfortable, even frightened, as if the unfortunate men weren't quite human. It was the first time I'd seen human casualties of war. The body bags I'd seen at the train site struck me as impersonal. These men made noises, laughed, joked, and talked.

Christine had warned me about what I was going to see. Seeing them had become a way of life for her, and she didn't appreciate the grim picture the men presented in seeing them for the first time. I found it particularly upsetting that most of the faces were young, few older than twenty.

I followed Christine along a path separating a second row of huts to one at the complex's end. What little space there was around the buildings had been turned into flowerbeds, all of an individual nature. Christine said the men took great pride in their gardening. Each hut competed with the next for the best flower array.

"Keeps them occupied," she said. "And also brightens up the place."

The end building had six beds, easy chairs, a large refectory table, a small kitchen, and toilet area. Between the beds was a table or workstation. Books, hand tools, paint pots, wood pieces, and paper littered the tables. Expertly produced aeroplane models hung from the ceiling. I recognized models of Hurricanes and Spitfires, our main fighter planes. They bore down on a formation of model German Messerschmitts and bombers.

At the far end of the room sat a four-foot-high model church made of matchsticks. Hanging above it was a hand-carved wooden crucifix. Painted on the wall to the right side was a half life-size portrait of a lady holding a baby. The baby had a golden halo surrounding its head. I'd seen a smaller similar picture in Christine's room. The whole room had an informal atmosphere, totally different from the hospital where I had my tonsils out.

Five men, older than most of the others I'd passed outside, but still in their late twenties or early thirties, greeted Christine and me. One was in a wheelchair with a blanket over his legs. Two men were on crutches—one had half his right leg missing. The two other men were lying on their beds with wheelchairs parked alongside. One had scars on the left side of his face and part of his hair was missing.

They were pleased to see Christine. She gave each a kiss on the cheek. As she introduced me, I only picked up two names. The man in the wheelchair was Lennie, and the tall man on crutches, who busied himself in the kitchen making tea and toast, was Michael.

It turned out they were Battle of Britain fighter pilots, all from the Free Polish Squadron who had escaped from the German invasion in their country. Their stories were legendary amongst us boys. They flew Hurricanes and had one wish: to kill Germans. After they lost their families, their homes, everything to the German invasion, they were known for being fearless, dedicated, and almost fanatical in their opposition to the Luftwaffe. They were magnificently brave to a point of recklessness. In battle, they filled the airwaves with what they regarded the dubious parentage of their opponents. They were called the mavericks of the skies. Few of their squadron survived the 1940 Battle of Britain, but their kill ratio was phenomenal. The Polish fighter squadron was credited with destroying no fewer than 120 German aircrafts in six weeks of fighting in 1940.

Here I was meeting five living legends in person. I was dumbstruck.

"Come here, John," one of the men lying on the bed said. "Let's have a look at you." He swung his dangling legs over the bedside and sat up. As he took hold of my waist and lifted me, I felt the power in his hands and arms. He stood me on his bed. "So this is the young man who has captured our Christine's heart," he said.

I coloured up and wondered what Christine had been saying about me.

From his wheelchair, Lennie suggested that we were rivals. His speech was heavily accented, but I understood every word.

"Rivals for what?" I asked.

"Christine's heart," he said with a grin. Everyone, including Christine, laughed.

"And the rest of us," another man added, and they laughed again.

Christine told them to behave themselves. "Show him around, why don't you," she suggested.

The men had used papier mâché to construct the model planes. They showed me how to use pulped, shredded newspaper mixed with flour and water to create one myself. I learnt to mold the pulp around a light wire frame. I realized it took days to go from pulp to the finished planes.

I got the pilots talking about aerial combat. Between eating toast and drinking tea, they demonstrated fighter techniques. The light shade high in the corner became the sun. We took the planes down from the ceiling. Christine, the pilots, and I held them. While standing or sitting around a bed, we flew an imaginary mission. It was spectacular to witness as each man maneuvered his plane, reliving his past. They spoke in Polish as if they were in radio contact. Michael, who spoke good English, translated the commands. Some outbursts he ignored. After they were satisfied the Messerschmitts and German bombers had been seen off or had perished, the pilots relaxed, and we had a second cup of tea and more toast.

I went with Lennie and Michael to the model cathedral. They told me they'd modeled it on a cathedral in Warsaw, Poland's capital. They made it from thousands of matches, each painstakingly glued together. They'd achieved highlighted areas by the skillful use of the matches' burnt ends.

Lennie and Michael were surprised I didn't know about the painting. They told me it was the Blessed Mother and Jesus. They were even further surprised when I didn't know what religion I was. They assumed, because of Christine, I was Catholic.

"What is a Catholic?" I asked.

They struggled to answer, but came up with faith, the pope, and Trinity—the Father and Son and the Holy Spirit. I wasn't much the wiser, but whatever being Catholic was, it meant a lot to Lennie and Michael.

"What religion are the Germans and Italians?" I asked.

They said many Germans and practically all Italians were Catholics. I was ready to ask if God took sides in the war, but Michael took me to see half-finished models of a German Junker and Stucker dive-bombers. In 1940, I'd seen a sky full of those feared planes heading for London.

A framed signed picture of an English pilot hung above the models. Both Michael and Lennie had met him. "Our inspiration," Michael said.

I'd seen a similar picture before. It was another air ace, Wing Commander Douglas Bader, a legless fighter pilot. His exploits and those of his fellow pilots made headlines in the newspapers. I knew he was a German prisoner of war.

When time came to leave, the pilots gave me a Spitfire model. After shaking their hands vigorously and waiting for Christine to do her rounds of cheek kissing, we waved good-bye at the door.

As Christine stopped to exchange greetings on the way out of the hospital, I saw the servicemen in a different light. Instead of feeling afraid, I felt comfortable and proud to be amongst them.

When Mother returned, Christine was glad for the company, and I for the cooking. Mother talked about how well my sister was doing. She hadn't made plans for her return, not until local schooling began.

Mother had two letters from Dad to open. He was "enjoying" himself somewhere in Italy. Mario, our Italian prisoner of war, was in England; and Dad, an Englishman, was in Italy. What irony.

Chapter 8

A PRESENT FOR HITLER

"Eight. Nine. Ten. One for luck, one extra for being cheeky." Christine and Mum had fun on my tenth birthday at my expense. They gave me the time-honored bumps, Christine holding my arms and Mum my legs. There was no doubt Christine was being vindictive. My backside hit the floor with a thump.

Christine was still mad at me. All I'd done was catch her going up the stairs in her short dressing gown.

I'd put my head around the corner, armed with my torch. "Who's got no knickers on?" I shouted, lighting her rump.

She let out a shriek, jumped three stairs onto the landing, and flew into her bedroom.

You would have thought I'd stuck my finger up her bum. I couldn't stop laughing. Got her back for coming into the bathroom, me in all my glory, I thought.

Oh, boy! Did I ever get the finger treatment later—her forefinger on my nose—and her full stare. "Never, never, never do that again!" she warned.

In the end, Christine cooled down, finally broke into a smile, and gave me a hug. "I suppose you're growing up fast," she said. "I'd better watch myself."

Still, she enjoyed helping Mother give me the bumps. They left me spread-eagled on the carpet. I'd put up a struggle, but bumps I was having. I lay there before having the last word. "Still got no knickers on," I said.

Christine feigned a kick at me before she burst out laughing, joined by Mother. She handed me my birthday present, a chocolate bar with two squares missing. "I love you," she said. "But not a whole month's ration worth." With Mother's guidance, she'd also knitted me a scarf with red-and-white stripes, the colours of the Arsenal Soccer team.

GranDad was one of their fervent supporters. He never missed a game. I had his souvenir programmes from the matches. I too was an Arsenal supporter, although I'd never been to a match. "Up the Arsenal," GranDad would say to anyone who'd listen. He'd give a blow-by-blow account of the latest game. If Arsenal won, someone played a blinder. If they lost, the referee or the linesmen was blind. "Offside, my arse!" he'd roar as if he could influence the result of a finished match.

Mother had knitted me a rolled-neck sweater with alternating gray and maroon rings, using wool from two old cardigans she'd unpicked. Christine said I looked like a furry animal in it. Mother said she was thinking of a skunk and added, "He'll probably smell like one after wearing it for a week." She turned to me and ordered, "For God's sake, try and keep this one clean."

Mother worried about my short pants. I had two pairs, both patched up so often, you couldn't tell what the originals looked like. I'd grown so much the pants were becoming positively indecent. A nursing friend of Mother's came to the rescue. Mum came home with two old pairs of grey short pants. They came down below my knees, and the belt hung around my navel, but growing and washing soon sorted out that problem.

The new scarf and sweater came in handy. January 1942 came in bleak and cold. The snow accumulation over a two-week period made access to the estate difficult. The delivery of already sparse supplies dropped to a trickle. Food became a problem. Mother made her own bread but eventually ran out of flour. She rationed me to two slices a day. It became staler and staler. We had margarine for the bread and what was left of the preserved jam. Our last two egg-producing ducks had gone. We'd eaten Chalky's rabbits, except for his four breeding does and bucks, over Christmas. There was no life in the pigpens down the road except for the odd sow carrying a litter.

Instead of bread, Mother carved up mangel-wurzels. Grown for feeding cattle and pigs, it was a cross between a turnip and a swede and about the size of a soccer ball. I was hungry and enjoyed their slightly sweet taste. Mother said they were good tummy fillers.

A stew pot continuously simmered on the cooker. What Mother added I didn't know, but I suspected it was only vegetables because I seldom found any meat. She managed to get hold of dog bones and livened it up a bit.

Christine had her own way of livening up mealtimes. She suspended an Oxo cube on a piece of string in the stew, counted up to ten, and took it out. After a month, it was no longer funny.

As the weather eased, horse-drawn cartloads of tinned food appeared. Much had been shipped from America. The tins were strictly rationed. Twice a week, Mother and I stood in a queue at the grocery store, waiting with our brown ration cards. Whatever was inside the tins invariably tasted the same. It had a thick tomato sauce or peculiar tasting gelatin, but it tasted good.

I developed a taste for one particular blend that turned up in the tins. Surprisingly, the only rationing of this delicacy was supply. When a cartload turned up, we could buy two or three at a time without using our food coupons. The concoction was called corned beef. I ate it sliced in sandwiches, mashed with potatoes and cabbage, and fried. For a special treat, Mother mixed it with flour and water until it resembled a thick pastry. She cut rounds, using an upturned breakfast cup, fried the rounds, and served them up with thick fried chips. It was Mother's version of steak and chips.

The radio, our contact with the outside world, boosted our morale. Production of planes, bombs, tanks, and trucks increased. The women, the larger part of our workforce, worked in shifts around the clock seven days a week.

Request music played continuously, dedicated to this or that production group, birthday, sweetheart, or husband. Vera Lynn's songs were popular. We heard her recordings of "We'll Meet Again" and "There'll Be Bluebirds over the White Cliffs of Dover" over and over. American band music was popular too, especially Glenn Miller's music. I'd walk down the street whistling "In the Mood" or "Little Brown Jug." It was a sad day when I heard that his plane crashed into the sea, and he had been killed on the way to a concert for the armed forces. Since he and Vera Lyn had become synonymous with wartime Britain, Glen Miller's death felt like a personal loss.

The news on the war front was good. We won the North African campaign, and Hitler didn't win the treasured oil route. The Allied forces advanced slowly into Italy. The Russians pushed the Germans back. The Italians caved in and joined the Allied forces in pushing the Germans out of Italy.

Mario delighted in the news. He was being moved on. Eventually, he hoped to return to Italy, where he was prepared to fight the Germans. He had no liking for Hitler. Whenever we discussed the war, he'd say Hitler's name and spit, unashamedly swearing in Italian.

The Americans and Allied forces steadily pushed the Japanese back. The tide had turned, as the papers put it. The end of the war was just a matter of time now.

The radio reported that the food and fuel shortage was improving because the German submarine U-boat threat to shipping in the Atlantic was diminishing. Some reports even suggested that the German offensive was over. This was premature however. Toward the end of January, the German Luftwaffe hit back and hit back hard. An eighteen-month period of relative calm came to an end.

The moaning minnies of air-raid sirens wailed again, day and night. I returned to sleeping under the stairs. Mother and Christine slept under the Morrison table.

News came through of a possible further blitz on London. Over two hundred bombers made a daylight raid. The bombers returned to Germany, reloaded and refueled and came back during the night. I heard and felt the heavy vibrating throb of planes overhead—ours or the enemy's, we had no way of knowing—and the pictures rattled on the wall.

If Christine was at work, Mother wanted me to keep her company under the Morrison table. When the planes passed overhead, she gripped me tightly. I clenched my fists. Sweat formed in my palms. We relaxed when the sounds died away.

The area around the estate didn't escape. Bombs dropped on the common and in the woods. Luckily, only one fell near enough to the estate to do damage. The shops lost their windows again as did houses to the top end of the estate. Epsom had three direct hits with over twenty fatalities reported, but many more required hospitalization.

A shot-down German bomber ploughed a path through the common near the church. Christine said it passed only a few feet above the hospital. Four enemy bombers fell in the wood and nearby downs. Chalky warned Ronnie and me to stay away from them for fear of an unexploded bomb.

The onslaught gradually receded over the next two months. London had improved defenses since 1940. The radio reported huge losses of German planes. Even so, we heard estimates of 1,500 civilians dead and 3,000 seriously injured each night. Hospitals filled up again. Many casualties were transported to where Mother and Christine worked. They, as many did, ignored the air-raid sirens and went to work as usual.

The cold weather continued into March. Coal supplies ran short. We lit a fire only of an evening to heat bathwater. Gradually, our coal ran out, and we had to make do with a kettle of hot water for washing.

Mother got extra khaki army blankets. I had two on my mattress over the eiderdown. Even so, it was still cold. I'd bury myself under the bedclothes, wearing my rolled-neck sweater and socks, breathing through a tunnel down the side of my pillow. In the mornings, when I took down the blackout curtains, I'd find a quarter inch of hoarfrost and had to scrape it off before I could see outside.

During the day, I wore two jumpers and two pairs of socks inside oversized Wellingtons. Over that, I wore a scarf, mittens, and a cut-down army trench coat. It wasn't fashionable, but I stayed warm.

The supply of electrical power was intermittent. Sometimes it would go off for hours and other times for a full day, but we had several periods of being without longer than two days.

By the end of March, the weather improved. Days warmed up to "one jumper" days when the chilling easterly wind died down. Coal supplies hadn't improved much, but we managed to get the odd sack. Mother and I risked going out while the sirens sounded off, pushing the pram into town to queue up at the coal merchant. The coal didn't last long, but it meant we could all have a bath twice a week. We used the same bathwater, but Christine insisted I bathe last.

I ignored the occasional daytime siren and went off into the woods. If I heard a siren, I'd lie flat on my stomach at a tree base. I'd bring back as large a piece of deadwood as I could carry. Cutting it up was a problem because my only tool was a blunt, rusty saw I found in the garden shed. Chalky tried to sharpen it for me. His saw wasn't any better. After working for a day, I produced a dozen logs and as many blisters. The logs helped, but we needed coal.

I had a flash of inspiration. Back in the autumn, Ronnie and I had walked up to the chalk downs to see the racehorses. On the way back, Ronnie dared me to walk across the brick parapet on the side of the railway bridge. At the centre, there was a thirty-foot drop to the railway line.

"You're chicken," he taunted.

"I dare you," I challenged.

"Not the point," he said. "I thought of it first. I bet you five marbles."

"You don't have five marbles," I countered.

He put a hand in his pocket and brought out a handful; two were big alleys.

"Where'd you get them?" I asked.

"Swapped them for a ferret."

"You ain't got a ferret," I said.

"Next door's ferret," he said. "They've left me to look after it while they're away."

"So you've swapped next door's ferret for some marbles? The ferret that don't belong to you?"

"A whole bag of marbles." Ronnie grinned.

"Reckon you've lost yours," I said.

"What?"

"Your marbles." I tapped my head. "What are you going to do when the neighbors come back?"

"Tell them it died, and I buried it," Ronnie said. "Now what about our bet?"

We settled the deal for five marbles and one big alley. The walk across the bridge parapet was easier than it looked. I noticed where trains stopped at the signals down the line. As they shunted off, the wagons heaped with coal shed some of their load. Coal pieces lay scattered alongside the railway tracks.

I won and doubled the bet by walking back again as a steam train, bellowing smoke, passed under the bridge.

When I remembered the coal at the railway tracks, I sounded Ronnie out. He was for it. Mother agreed probably because she was desperate. We convinced her that we could make the public air-raid shelter at the top of the estate if the situation became serious. We set off that evening at dusk with Mother's good wishes, a "Be careful" and the pram.

For several nights, we did well, collecting a pram full of coal and sharing it between us. Mum was anxious while we were gone and always pleased to see us return. Gradually, the gleaning dried up. We had nearly cleaned up both sides of the track and figured that was our last night for a while. It was also the night we got caught.

A voice rang out, "What the bleeding hell do you think you're doing down there?" The shadowy figure of a man stood on the lower rails of the embankment fence.

"What now?" Ronnie asked.

My mind raced. We could escape by running up the other side of the embankment, but that meant leaving the pram. Mum wouldn't be pleased. No, we had to face him.

Ronnie had other ideas. "We could throw coal at him," he suggested. "He might go away."

"I need the pram, Ronnie," I told him. "We can't take a chance. Anyhow, we're doing sod all harm. Let's go and face him."

"Coming up," I shouted to the man. "Just coaling."

Ronnie held a coal lump in each hand and followed me up the embankment. When we got there, the man started on his Magna Carta, "Don't you know that's private property? It's dangerous. You're trespassing. Could get killed. You're thieving. Damn brats, the pair of you. Be off before I take my hand to you!"

I thought I'd like to see him try. I also had a sizeable coal chunk clenched in my right hand. "Just picking up waste coal," I said. "We're doing no harm. And there's no danger. We can hear a train coming from miles away."

He went off again with his tirade, punctuating each utterance with a swear word. We didn't bother to argue anymore and left quickly.

Later we realized the man wasn't genuine. He was scruffy and unshaven, and he had shifty eyes. He didn't even ask our names or where we lived. We doubted his authority. He just wanted us to clear off. What for, we wondered. There was something strange going on. It smelled. We decided to go back and investigate.

We crept back quietly to the railway embankment. A horse and cart stood tied up to the embankment fence. A train had stopped at the signals. Peering through the half-light, we saw two silhouettes on top of the coal trucks. They worked fast, shoveling coal onto the side of the embankment. As the train steamed up, ready to move off, the men jumped down. We moved a safe distance back across the green and put the pram on its side. Lying in the long grass, we waited. The men appeared, each carrying a sack of coal they loaded on the cart. Every three or four minutes, they appeared with another two sacks. After a while, the cart had twenty sacks.

We heard one man say, "Last two to go. A good night's work."

"Come on," I said to Ronnie. "Grab the pram."

Ronnie started to question me, but I stopped him. "No questions. Just grab the other end of the pram and come with me." He followed me to the cart.

"Up!" I said, and we threw the pram on top of the coal sacks.

Ronnie jumped up on the cart's tailgate. "Thought you were just going to pinch a sack," he whispered.

"Why one?" I whispered back. "May as well have the bloody lot."

I jumped into the driver's seat, took off the hand brake, and gave the reins a flick. We moved off to the bridge and turned left onto the road leading up to the top entrance of the estate. After we'd gone a hundred yards or so,

I heard the men shouting. I broke the horse into a canter, putting my farm training to good use. Ronnie shouted from the back, "Coal for sale, two shillings a sack."

I drove the horse and cart out past the top entrance to the estate, across the common, and into the bracken. We struggled to unload the sacks. Once we finished, I turned the horse and cart around, and we headed back to the estate entrance. After telling Ronnie to jump, I gave the horse a whack with the loose end of the rein and jumped myself. The horse and cart carried on into the direction of the estate. Ronnie and I walked the long way around to our houses.

Chalky came around the next day. He said one of his fellow air-raid workers found a horse and cart wandering around the estate last night. It wasn't until midday they found the owners, a couple of totters. "Up to no good," Chalky said. "Told us the horse and cart had been stolen from outside a friend's house they'd been visiting. Likely tale. Who'd pinch a horse and cart? Too easily recognized. They've been warned not to be on the estate without reason."

I smiled with relief.

Ronnie and I waited a couple of nights until we got our nerves back. Then we prammed the coal home each evening. It lasted until regular supplies came through.

There had been no daylight bombing for three weeks when Mother said I could start school again at a temporary school in a church hall at the edge of town. A retired headmaster planned to run it. Boys aged ten to twelve could attend between nine o'clock and twelve thirty. Afternoons were for younger boys. I had to take a jam jar with me for milk during morning break. Tin mugs were in short supply. The few we had at home had long since replaced the broken china cups.

I told Ronnie's mother about the school, and Mother filled in the details. Once she knew about it, she insisted Ronnie go too.

Ronnie wasn't very keen on it. "Daft thing to tell my mother," he said. "I'm going to beat you up for this."

"You can try," I said.

It was bluff and double bluff.

Ronnie cheered by up the morning school started. We met at the top of the estate for our walk into town. My bicycle inner tubes had long given up the struggle to retain air. No amount of patching worked. Soapy water and inflation revealed more holes than Ronnie's stories.

As we came to the houses across the common, we caught up with two other boys. Ronnie knew them because they'd been evacuated to the same town. One was named Bonker; the other Kelly. Both were twelve years old.

Bonker, like me, was tall for his age, an inch taller than me and a good two inches taller than Kelly, who was nearly as wide as he was tall. His baggy short pants couldn't hide the size of his backside. His face was large and round, sitting on a squat neck like a fairground boxer. The green-and-orange school cap did nothing for him either. Kelly was the only one of us to bring sandwiches to school, but he ate them along the way. He reminded me of Billy Bunter, a character in one of the comic annuals I had at home. Billy Bunter's appetite and quest for food were fun reading, but he always ended up on the sticky end of his conniving to obtain food.

Bonker was well built but not fat. His stocky frame supported a head full of short dark brown curly hair. There was something familiar about his features, and I realized they were similar to Jed's, one of the boys who taught me to fight at Talgarth.

"You were with my cousin at Talgarth," he said. "Some scrapper, I hear. Jed told me you lived up on the estate. He went up to try to find you once."

They'd been moved to a hotel near Abergavenny and lived with forty other boys. They worked the land during the days and received an education during the evenings. "It was tough," said Bonker. "But we had some fun. They came back the end of last summer, same as Kelly and me." He said Stan and Jed had been drafted to work in a munitions factory near Coventry.

I shuddered as I remembered seeing pictures of the Coventry bombing. Neither Stan nor Jed could wait until next year. They both wanted to join the army.

We found a tin can at the roadside and kicked it to each other as we walked to school. Kelly didn't say much, but when he did, it was with difficulty. He had a bad stutter.

Before reaching the main road leading out of town, Kelly and Bonker parted company with us. They were taking a shortcut across an expanse of waste grassland. Tank traps crisscrossed the land, full of water and weeds. Dilapidated signs, warning "Mines, Keep Out," didn't deter Kelly and Bonker.

"Codswallop," Bonker said. "A load of nonsense. There are no mines."

The grass was long and wet. Neither Ronnie nor I wore Wellingtons, so we took the long way around.

At the corner of the road was a pillbox. Ronnie couldn't resist it. He jumped up onto the blast wall, using a gun slit to help him climb onto the flattop. "Rat-a-tat-tat," he sounded, arms outstretched, pretending to machine-gun the passersby on the other side of the road. They ignored him.

I hunched over and walked through the pillbox entrance behind the blast wall. What a mistake! It was a public toilet. No, worse than that. It had never been cleaned. Putrefied turds and stained newspapers were everywhere. The stench made me gasp. It was repulsive. At least, it wasn't summer with flies, bluebottles, and maggots. I left quickly. The Germans could have our pillboxes. I wished we could send one to Hitler, parcel it up, and post it to him for his birthday. "To Hitler, the only bit of England you're going to get. Love, Churchill."

The school hall was about two hundred yards from the pillbox. On the way, I asked Ronnie about Kelly and Bonker. "How come Kelly's so fat on rations? Are his mum and dad large?"

"His mum's large but not fat," Ronnie said. "Don't know about his dad. They lost him at the start of the war. He'll eat anybody's leftovers at school dinners."

"He must have been hungry," I said, remembering our school dinners delivered in black containers. They were lukewarm if we were lucky, cold if you were more than a third of the way down the queue. We got green cabbage or swede with everything. Friday was sick day. Lumps—supposed to be fish—swam in fat in a greyish sauce. Boys won bets by eating second helpings. The winners usually got sick afterward, bringing up a warmer version of what went in.

Ronnie said, "Kelly's real forename is Cuthbert. He hates it. Prefers to be called by his surname. If you want to annoy him, call him Cuthbert."

"Who would want to be called Cuthbert?" I asked. "Sounds like a pounced-up poodle. Nobody could accuse Kelly of looking like that."

I wondered how Bonker got his name. Ronnie said, "In the playground. The local boys goaded him into a fight because he was the biggest of us. Bonk. Bonk. They ended up flat on their backs. After that, he was Bonker." Ronnie added, "His dad is away in the navy."

When we got to the church hall late, the headmaster gave us a stare over half-lensed spectacles. "Names?" he asked. After we gave our names, he said, "Sit yourselves down. Don't be late again."

The church hall was laid out in rows of refectory tables, two tables to each row butted together, and collapsible wooden chairs. We found pencils, paper, and notebooks on the tables. We sat in the spare seats in the middle of the fifth row. Kelly and Bonker sat to our left on the end of the fourth row. Forty boys filled the hall.

The headmaster stood in front of a desk with a large blackboard behind him and a smaller one to his left. He had written instructions on the small blackboard: write our names, dates of birth, addresses, and the seat numbers located on our chair back. Unless otherwise instructed, these were our assigned seats.

He was tall, well built, and almost portly. A man in his late fifties, he wore a well-groomed grey moustache and a short haircut, which made his head look too big. His graying lightly greased hair parted in the middle. The jacket of his dark three-piece suit hung over a chair. A watch and chain strung across the lower pockets of his waistcoat. A dark square-knotted tie hung from his starched-stiff collar. He protected his shirt cuffs and lower sleeves with black-cloth forearm coverings similar to those I'd seen on bank tellers. A Scotsman with a deep voice and a heavy accent, his name was Mr. MacDonald. Out of earshot, we called him Big Mac. He peered at us over his spectacles, collected our papers, and started class. We stood up straight and recited the Lord's Prayer. Few of us knew it, so he wrote it on the board for us to copy.

"Stuff it," Ronnie said. "I thought I was coming to school, not church."

"No talking at the back," Big Mac barked.

Next we had to write for half an hour, telling Big Mac about the best day we could remember. "Fill two pages," he said.

I decided to write about the farm and helping Owen. After a page and a half of listing the animals, I struggled. Ronnie sat with his arms folded. He had written two lines. I looked over his shoulder and read, "The best day I had was in bed with a cold reading my komics."

"You can't hand that in," I whispered.

"Why not?" he asked. "It's all I could think of."

"Comics is spelled with a c, not a k," I said.

"Know-it-all," he taunted, but he changed the k to a c.

While I was thinking about what to add to my work, I folded a paper aeroplane. Ronnie grabbed it from me and winged it down the hall. Up it went, turned over, and sailed on until it clanked it against the blackboard. Big Mac had been walking around the hall, looking over boys' shoulders. He was two rows in front as the plane passed his head.

"Who did that?" He spun around.

Ronnie pointed at Kelly. The boys in back caught on and pointed at Kelly. Poor Kelly. He tried to protest, but the words wouldn't come out. The headmaster told him to go and stand in the corner on the stage, facing the wall. Big Mac went to his desk and brought out a long thin willowy cane. Whack! He crashed it on the desk. Whack! We were still as tombs. I worried Kelly would get a whacking.

"I expect this is what most of you are used to," the headmaster said. "How many strokes?" He pointed at Kelly.

"Six," said a depraved soul at the front. Kelly's backside must have been twitching. Mine was.

Ronnie jumped to his feet. "It was me, sir, not him."

"Ah, the mice are coming out of the woodwork," said Big Mac as he gave Ronnie a long stare. "Sit down," he told Kelly to return to his seat. Big Mac waved the cane again. "Six of the best sounds like this." He whacked the table six times.

We winced at the sound.

"Do you like getting the cane?" He surveyed the hall.

We shook our heads. My lips went dry.

"Good," he said. "Never used one. Never had to. There are other ways." He broke the cane over his knee and put the halves in the waste bin.

After school, Kelly stank. He admitted to creaming his pants. We made him walk home downwind of us. Kelly was mad. He wanted to thump Ronnie, but we persuaded him that it was a joke that backfired. It was Big Mac who was the joker though. He had fooled us all.

Big Mac's discipline was quite simple. Messing around or not paying attention got a stint in the corner. Three stints in the corner and you missed the Friday treat. He gave us a sample of the Friday treat. He covered the large blackboard with a white sheet and asked the boys nearest the windows to pull down the blackout curtains while he took a dustcover off a projector. He flipped off the lights. We saw a Charlie Chaplin film, the first one I'd ever seen.

On Fridays the boys who behaved themselves could watch a one-hour film show at the end of the morning session. Most of us had one stint in the corner. Several had two. No one made three.

School became fun. Big Mac interspersed lessons with talks of his travels. Sometimes he discussed war news. His stories had a point that led into a new exercise.

The visit to the corner or sin bin, as we called it, had its moments. The walls we faced had aged from a dark cream to a dirty brown color. While

Big Mac addressed the class, whoever was in the sin bin quickly wrote a rhyme or perverse statement on the wall. To read the messages, you had to cock your head just right to catch the light on the graphite. The messages told about who was well hung, whose sister would drop them for two cigarettes, the doubtful parentage of Big Mac, and what Nell—whoever she was—would do with your privates. Being in the sin bin wasn't boring. It was stimulating reading.

Kelly gave the game away though. One day, while sitting in the sin bin, he snorted with laughter, his head bowed and shoulders heaving. Big Mac stopped his lesson and perused the walls for two full minutes, stooping, turning his head this way and that, catching the light. We were absolutely silent. We held our breaths. Undoubtedly, the film show was out for a week, at least, but we wandered what else he would do.

The headmaster took his time walking back to his desk and then turned slowly and gazed at us over his spectacles, one row at a time. I avoided eye contact with him. Ronnie put his hands over his head and laid his forehead on the refectory table and mumbled, "It's a nightmare. I will be somewhere else when I wake up."

"Wait for it," I whispered. "Here it comes. He's going to speak."

"I see we have a glimmer of talent in the class," Big Mac said at last. "I was beginning to give up hope. Been years since I've seen anything new." Then came the sting. "A pity to spoil good prose with such poor spelling. I think we should do something about that." He filled the large blackboard with words that we copied in our notebooks. "Monday morning," he paused. "A meaning-and-spelling test. Anybody with more than five wrong is for the high jump."

What high jump meant I wasn't sure, but it sounded mean. He'd written twenty-five words on the blackboard, and I was taking no chances. I planned to work on them over the weekend using the dictionary. Mother could test me Sunday night. I wondered what she would make of testicles, prostitution, and pervert as spelling words.

As for Kelly, his outburst in the sin bin cost him half an hour after school scrubbing down the walls.

Toward the end of March, I saw soldiers cleaning the bracken and putting in wide gravel tracks that crisscrossed the common. Nobody on the estate knew what was going on, not even Chalky. Anyhow, he was preoccupied.

He had taken to riding his bicycle out, dressed in a pinstriped suit, a waistcoat, a white shirt with stiff white collar, and a thin dark tie. He polished his boots and wore a bowler hat. If the day was fine, he strapped his coat and umbrella over the crossbar. I had never seen Chalky in formal dress before.

Mother said he was courting a widow with two daughters who lived across the common in one of the cottages. Chalky met her a year ago, and they were planning to get married. He wanted me to be the pageboy.

Mum said I was going to be the pageboy, like it or not.

Mum knew Chalky's intended. She was a Sister on one of the wards where Mother worked. "She's a lovely lady," Mother said. "Just right for Chalky."

The day of the wedding came around quickly but not without some fuss beforehand. Mother produced a light brown pageboy suit, or monkey suit as I called it, and altered it to fit me. If the suit wasn't bad enough, a frilly shirt arrived along with a silk handkerchief, a brown-and-cream spotted bow tie, and a pair of used but highly polished brown boots. I protested, but she said I had to wear the lot and stop whinging.

"Chalky has done a lot for us," she said. "It's the least you can do."

Ronnie came around during the fitting. He collapsed on the floor, laughing.

The wedding was at the church near the hospital. I went to the rehearsal two days before. I had to walk behind Chalky's new missus, holding the end of a draped curtain pinned to her dress back.

She was an attractive lady with a bright face and laughing eyes. Her teenage daughters, the bridesmaids, giggled during the rehearsal. They teased me and pinched my bottom as we walked down the aisle. They insisted on kissing me and smeared lipstick all over my face. I found a frog in the church graveyard and chased them around the vestry with it.

On the morning of the wedding, I dressed in my monkey suit an hour before time to leave for the church. Mum plastered my hair down with Brylcreem. When the doorbell rang, Mother shouted for me to answer. There stood Ronnie, Kelly, and Bonker. Kelly and Bonker didn't believe Ronnie's story about my outfit, so they came to see for themselves. It was going to take a while to live this down. My street credibility had been severely damaged, and I had to put up with "Pansy John will give you a thrill" for weeks afterward.

Mother and Christine were still in their dressing gowns. They took turns doing each other's hair. Fingernails got a coat of red lacquer, and then fingers waved in front of the fire. The powder puff worked gently over their faces and necklines. Two dabs of powder went on Christine's nose, but she was sure it was still shiny. I got a powder dab on my nose because I laughed. The rouge on their cheeks was a work of art, just enough to give a healthy appearance.

"Too much and you'll look like a tart," Mother said to Christine.

They applied mascara on their eyelashes and penciled their eyebrows. Finally, they applied deep red lipstick. Neither Christine nor Mother had ever worn much makeup. The transformations were remarkable.

"War paint," Mother said to me. "How do we look?"

I gave a nod of approval.

After a flick of the hair here and adjustments with a comb there, they went upstairs to dress.

There was another loud knock on the door.

"Answer it," Mother shouted down the stairs. "If it's your mates again, tell them to hop it. You're not going anywhere."

I opened the door. Standing on the doorstep was a young lad dressed in a grey tunic with a red stripe down the side of his trousers. He was a post office telegram messenger boy. I knew they were bearers of war office telegrams stating, "It is with regret," followed by the words missing, prisoner of war or worse, killed in action. I'd seen them on the estate and watched—with my fingers crossed—and breathed a sigh of relief when they cycled past our house. Drawn curtains and flower wreaths invariably followed their visits.

"Telegram," he said to me. "Please sign here."

I signed and closed the door, walked through the dining room, placed it on the table, and plopped in a chair. I heard Mother and Christine laughing upstairs.

"John, who was it?" she called down.

I didn't answer.

"John, who was it?" she repeated.

I got up slowly, walked to the bottom of the stairs, and called, "A telegram boy. We have a telegram."

Mother and Christine, still in their dressing gowns, rushed downstairs. I pointed to the telegram. Mother picked it up, but put it down again. She sat down. "I can't open it," she said. "Will you do if for me, Christine?"

Christine took a deep breath, put her finger in the flap, and split the envelope open. Slowly she unfolded the telegram. She read it to herself and let out a whoop. "It's from your husband. Terrific news."

HAVE BEEN GIVEN R AND R STOP
BACK IN ENGLAND IN FEW DAYS STOP
BE HOME FOR A WHILE STOP
SEND DETAILS LATER STOP.

Mother leapt from the chair and grabbed Christine. They danced around the room, laughing and crying at the same time. They reached out to me, and I joined them in jigging around the room. Finally, Christine and Mother flopped into our two easy chairs. Tears of joy flooded out. Mascara streaked their faces. I went to the bathroom and returned with two hand towels.

Christine wiped her face and said, "I think we could do with a cup of tea." She left to put on the kettle.

Mother pulled me onto her lap. She wrapped her arms around my neck and gave me two kisses on the cheek.

Over tea, I asked, "What's R and R?"

"Rest and recuperation," she said. "We're going to kick up our heels." She picked up a hand mirror and glanced into it. She laughed and handed the mirror to Christine.

"I've some serious patching to do," Christine said.

Christine passed the mirror to me. "You too," she said.

I had two smudges of lipstick on my cheek, but I didn't really care. Dad was safe. Mother was happy.

After a hurried and final preening by Christine and Mother, we were ready to go to the church. Mother looked elegant in a ruby dress. Christine looked stunning in a flame velvet dress borrowed from their fellow nurses at the hospital. Wide-brimmed hats, also borrowed, completed their outfits.

"This dress has been to six weddings," Christine said.

Mum said she looked like a princess in it, and I agreed. I was proud to be with them. I did persuade Mother to let me wear my coat on the way to church even though it was a warm day, so I'd look normal.

There were over a hundred and fifty people in the congregation, many nurses and men in uniform.

The walk down the aisle went off well. I kept the three yards of wedding dress train waist high at my end, so the centre was six inches above the floor, while keeping in step with the bride and escort. The dress was made of parachute silk as were the bridesmaids' dresses; one dyed a primrose yellow, the other a dark rose pink. The bridesmaids behaved themselves this time.

Chalky wore a full army dress uniform. He looked splendid with his three rows of campaign ribbons and a row of medals.

I had to stand until halfway through the ceremony. Now and then, Mother whispered from her aisle seat, "Stand up straight" or "Stop picking your nose."

After the vows, Chalky's Home Guard and air-raid warden friends, all in full military dress, formed the guard of honour. They made an arch of swords as the couple exited the church. In the austerity that normally surrounded us, the wedding was an oasis. Even a photographer was at hand with a plate camera and an assistant to hold an acetylene lamp. Chalky and his new wife must have been well-thought-of because everyone had gone to a great deal of trouble to make the wedding a special occasion.

Four full-dressed Scots pipers led the wedding procession out of the churchyard and across to the hospital grounds, where a buffet reception was laid on. Despite my protests about what I had to wear, Chalky's wedding was a fine day.

Mother and Christine got tiddly on elderberry wine. Halfway home, Christine took off her satin shoes and challenged me to a race up the asphalted path.

After the wedding, Chalky closed up his house and went to live across the common. Although he visited occasionally, we missed him.

Late the following morning, Ronnie came around bursting with news. "The Yanks are here!"

"The Yanks?"

"Americans, stupid."

"How do you know?"

"On the common," he said. "Putting up tents."

"How do you know they're Americans?" I asked.

"Their hair looks like stubbled corn and they're all chewing gum," he said, not bothering to say they were dressed in distinctive uniforms and flew the American flag on their Jeeps and lorries.

I wanted to rush out to see them, but Mother said I had to eat first. Ronnie stayed for lunch. Because his mother worked all day, he had to fend for himself. I told Ronnie the news about my father.

"Great," he said without emotion.

"Great?" I repeated, expecting more from him.

"Sorry." He got up and gave me a pat on the shoulder. "Made me think of my dad is all. He won't be coming back." His eyes were moist, most unlike him.

He didn't have much, not even a radio at home. His mother worked long hours and wasn't home until nine o'clock some nights. If he turned up with something, he had bartered for it or got it in some dubious way. He lived by his wits. Nobody could blame him if he was miserable and bemoaned his luck, but usually he was cheerful, quick with a laugh.

Mother brought us two steaming plates of stew, dumplings, and mashed potatoes. "Got something for you, Ronnie," she said, reaching into her workbasket. It was a wool rolled-neck sweater with alternating dark and light blue horizontal stripes. I was sure she had been knitting it for me, but I kept quiet. Instinctively, I understood.

Ronnie jumped up, leaving his dinner, pulled off his old tattered jumper, and pulled on the new sweater. He beamed.

"It's your birthday in the week, isn't it?" Mother said.

"Not for another week," he said. "But I can keep it, can't I?"

"Of course," she said.

Lunch over, Ronnie and I set off to see the Yanks.

Chapter 9

YANKS JOIN THE LAND ARMY

From our perch forty feet above the common in the largest of the Douglas firs, Ronnie and I had a great view of the Yanks. We saw convoys of lorries and jeeps carrying men and supplies. The vehicles had pendants on their wings, displaying the American flag and a white pentagon star painted on the doors. We'd seen the same star on the wings of the familiar Mustang P-51 fighter planes and the Flying Fortress B-17 bombers.

Lines of camouflaged teepee tents went up quickly, with larger marquis tents in the centre. Flights of aircraft passed overhead. They must have been ours because we didn't hear a siren or ack-ack flack. Barrage balloons stretched out in the distance toward London.

Several jeeps towed Bofors antiaircraft guns. Others towed searchlights fixed onto generators. We saw guns and searchlights set up in clearings amongst the bracken and gorse bushes. Camouflage netting covered all stationary equipment. Even the paths appeared a natural part of the countryside, providing shortcuts across the common to the fields and town.

When two Mustangs flew past low, dipping their wings while passing over the camp, we nearly fell out of the tree. The American soldiers whistled and waved in return.

We spotted Kelly and Bonker in the path, so we waved and whistled to attract their attention. Kelly decided to climb the tree. What a pantomime! The first bough was about seven feet up. Ronnie and I had used foot—and handholds in the rough bark to level ourselves into the tree. Not Kelly.

128

We helped him onto Bonker's shoulders. Then Ronnie and I, perched on the lower bough, managed to pull him up. He was some weight! Twenty feet up, he decided that was enough. We left him there and climbed to the top.

Kelly tried to get a better view by inching his way out a sturdy bough, using a branch above to steady himself. In slow motion—we shouted because we saw it coming—the bough bent over, and Kelly lost his grip. He slid down and off the end of the fanned-out branch, a twenty-foot drop, but his luck held. It was amazing sight. He landed smack in the middle of a bramble bush, spread-eagled on his back, creating a huge crater in the bush and suspended several feet off the ground. Kelly had bombed a bramble bush. Now we had to get him out.

On the ground, the bush looked more formidable than from high in the tree. Kelly was in about eight feet, clucking away like a blackbird. The brambles were dense, a good half-inch thick, and the thorns were large and hardened from several years' growth.

Ronnie had the first idea. Reaching into his Aladdin's cave of pockets, he came out with matches. "Let's set fire to the bush and put the fire out just before it reaches him."

Both Bonker and I turned on him. "Stupid! You can't do that."

Ronnie looked at us, then at the bush, scratched his head, and said, "Nope. I suppose you're right. The bush is damp as well as green. Won't catch easily. Right then. What's your idea?"

Bonker shook his head in disbelief. When Kelly heard Ronnie's idea, his clucking sounded like ten blackbirds.

An American jeep drew up with four soldiers all dressed in olive drab overalls. "Hi, boys. Locals?"

"Yes," Ronnie said. "Got any gum?"

"Funny accents," Bonker said in my ear.

"Have you a spade or an axe?" I asked, pointing into the bush. The clucking had gone quiet.

The soldiers looked at the bush, puzzled. One hopped out of the jeep and walked up to the bush, looking into the branches. He turned around and grinned. "Gee, fellows. These little buggers have thrown their buddy into the bush."

We laughed. The very idea of being able to throw Kelly anywhere was a joke. I explained what happened. In no time, the four soldiers got folding spades from the jeep and chopped their way into Kelly and lifted him out. Except for scratches, he was fine. We thanked them on Kelly's behalf—he was still clucking on about being roasted alive—and tried to pacify him by telling him that Ronnie could have asked for petrol instead of gum.

The soldiers produced gum, two sticks each, wrapped in pale yellow grease-proofed paper. Ronnie was happy. It was my first taste of gum. Magic! An everlasting sweet. Nearly. It lasted three days pinned behind my ear when not in use.

The soldiers asked our names and introduced themselves. Joe seemed to be in charge. He did most of the talking and had the look of authority. His confident blue eyes fixed on me as he spoke. He was a tall man, in his midtwenties. He reminded me of the hero in a Western film Big Mac had run, fast on the draw, quick with his fists, winning against all odds. He also spoke in the same deep, slow drawl.

Marvin—Marv for short—was Joe's right-hand man. He was a mountain of a man, older than Joe by five or six years. He was lean but huge. He would have had to stoop to come through our front door. His hands were the size of dinner plates, and his neck thicker than my thighs. His large square weather-beaten face and red hair made him look even more formidable.

"How would you like to tackle him?" I asked Bonker.

"Not without a Sherman tank," he said.

When Marv laughed, his face melted into a wide boyish grin.

"Gentle giant," Joe said.

The other two, Ed and Mitch, were heavy, thickset men, slightly shorter than Joe. They had features similar to Mario, the Italian prisoner of war, with their dark brown flashing eyes and black hair. Two days of black stubble on their faces didn't improve their appearance. I wouldn't want to meet them on a dark night.

"Commandos?" Ronnie asked, taking an interest in something other than the pistols the soldiers wore and the guns racked up in the jeep.

"Special forces," Joe said.

"Similar," Marv added. His eyes went spooky before he smiled. "They are silent-in-the-night throat-slitters."

Mitch gave Marv a friendly punch in the belly. "Knock it off. You'll scare the living daylights out of these babes," he said.

"Don't look like they scare easy," Joe said. "Where do things go on around here? Any dances, local pubs? Where's the action?"

We didn't know about dances, but Bonker pointed across to the left-hand path, directing them down to the cricket green and duck pond. "There's a public house there called the Cricketeers."

"Good," Marv said. "Town is out of bounds for most of the guys."

"Cricket?" Ed said. "Isn't that the game where grass growing is the fastest action? How do you play it?"

Bonker nearly exploded. Cricket was his passion. His dad played professionally before the war. Cricket was not a conversation to start with Bonker. He never stopped talking about it. He took the bait while Ed held the line.

In no time, two stones became wickets and other stones became fielders. Bowling leg breaks, off breaks, googlies came out. They discussed fielding positions of square leg, short leg, and gully. At silly mid-on, Ed stopped Bonker in midflow.

"Now let's take a look at this," Ed said. "A fielder stands six feet in front of the bat. The rock-solid ball travels at ninety miles an hour. The batter hits the ball as hard as he likes. That chap stands there with no padding or protection."

"That's right," Bonker said. "He's supposed to catch the ball."

"What's his position again?"

"Silly mid-on," Bonker said, gleeful at making a convert.

"It looks suicide to me," Ed said.

"No," Bonker insisted, moving another stone. "Suicide's there."

Joe butted in and asked, "How many watch this game?"

"A big game—seventy thousand or more," Bonker said.

"Now let me see," Joe added. "It lasts five days?"

Bonker nodded.

Joe counted on his fingers. "Five days. Seventy thousand people at two bucks a day, plus soda and popcorn. Still don't understand it, but it sounds a fine game to me." Joe checked his watch and climbed into the jeep. The others followed. With a parting comment of "See you around," they left for the camp.

"Did you see that?" Ronnie asked.

"See what?" I said.

"They had machine guns and ammunition in the back." His eyes were wide as he spoke.

We were going to have to keep an eye on Ronnie. He was lethal with a catapult. Rooks and crows could testify to that. Bonker was still looking at his stones, resetting his field, heavily involved in an imaginary game. Kelly was busy taking thorns out of his ample backside. We gave him a hand, picking them off his back. The school cap he wore had protected his head.

The air-raid siren sounded off. We didn't see anything in the sky, didn't hear the sound of planes, so we figured it was another false warning. We decided to head for home.

Air-raid observers, even with powerful binoculars, had trouble distinguishing between the Luftwaffe Messerschmitt 109 and the American Air Force Mustang P-51. They were similar in size and contour. Because of the many false air-raid warnings, people began to ignore them, particularly in daytime.

Heavy clouds came in on Monday, intermingled with spasms of bright sunshine, typical of April. The clouds brought a fret, a fine misty rain. It felt like standing too close to a waterfall.

I told Mother my right shoe was leaking because of a hole in the sole. I had no other shoes. My Wellingtons didn't fit me. She said I'd have to make do by using a thick cardboard insole she cut from a box. The insole lasted for an hour. I had a wet foot for three days.

Finally, Mother got a pair of small army boots. They were terrific. They had metal round studs in the soles and steel heels and toe caps. They were a bit large, but two pairs of woolen socks sorted that out.

The weather dried up at the end of the week. Mother had great news to go with the bright sunshine. Dad would be home on Sunday, either midafternoon or early evening, depending on the trains.

She also heard from GranDad who had been busy the last three months, living almost permanently in an air-raid shelter. He hoped to get down for the following weekend to see us.

Christine was in high spirits. There was a dance on Saturday night at the hospital. The nurses were excited because the American officers arranged with the hospital to lay on a meal. The Yanks were providing everything else, including a live band and forty live officers.

"Months since I've been to a dance," Christine said. "I wonder what Americans are like."

"Same as any other fellows," Mother said with a wink. "Sure you be careful."

"What do I wear?" Christine asked.

With that, the panic started. Mother cleaned the house, and Christine raided hers and Mother's wardrobes.

Friday was a waste of time at school. Twice we filed across the road to a public air-raid shelter only for the all clear to sound twenty minutes later. Big Mac sent us off early without a film show.

We paid the Yanks a visit, taking the long way around over the hill past the cricket green, arriving in the woods on the edge of the common.

A German bomber had ploughed a long, wide furrow in the trees and come to an abrupt end, transforming the woods. We found an odd piece of a wing, a badly mangled empennage, the cockpit, and a quarter of the fuselage. The plane's remnants were badly charred, suggesting that it had exploded and caught fire on impact. We wondered if the crew got out alive, but it didn't look possible. Ronnie satisfied himself that there was no treasure trove, and we continued.

We ran into a party of American soldiers who let us watch as they built an assault course through the woods. They strung up climbing nets and piled up logs to provide a ramp with a sheer drop to the other side. They filled over with earth a long low tunnel made with timber props and beams. We saw ropes dangling off tree boughs. They felled a tree to provide a crossing over a wide, deep trough cut by a stream.

After we left, a platoon of soldiers came running past us, chanting a song in rhythm to their running. We joined in with one group, Bonker and I holding Kelly's hands, but gave up when Kelly fell over for the third time.

At the entrance to their camp, two armed guards blocked our way. "No pass, no entrance." They had strung rolls of barbed wire around the camp. It didn't matter whom we knew. Civilians weren't allowed in, not without a pass anyhow. "Sorry, rules are rules," a guard said. "Go and get into mischief somewhere else." We did.

Farther down the compound, we saw a stack of fifty-gallon oil drums camouflaged by netting thrown loosely over the stack. The drums were empty. Ronnie came up with a brain wave. We each took hold of a drum and rolled it down the grass track until we came to a large bomb crater full of water. Bonker and I looked for timber planks at an abandoned building site while Ronnie looked for rope. We were successful, and so was Ronnie. He had two clotheslines.

"How did you get those?" I asked even though I knew the answer.

"Don't worry," he said. "They weren't using them."

"Is one of those my mother's?" I asked.

"I'm not that daft," he said. "Your mother's line had washing on it."

We had four oil drums and four planks bound tightly with washing lines, so we made ourselves a raft.

"I name this ship Epsom Salts," stuttered Kelly, peeing on the raft. With that, we set sail across the bomb crater, armed with loose fencing planks Ronnie had found.

Saturday was taken up with the raft. We found old pants to use as swimming trunks. The water was very cold, but we soon got used to it. The raft became a diving platform.

Arriving home for tea, I found the household in a stir. Christine hogged the bathroom for over an hour, so I had to go down behind the garden shed for a pee. Upstairs and downstairs went Christine, asking, "How does this look? How does that look?" Finally, she decided on a long navy pleated skirt, a white blouse, and a cherry red cardigan that Mum knitted. Mother let Christine borrow a string of pearls. She had borrowed a pair of black shiny high-heeled shoes from someone.

"Is the king going to be at this dance?" I asked.

"Shut up," she said. "No more of your cheek."

"Were you like this?" I asked Mother while Christine was on her umpteenth trip upstairs.

"Of course," she said. "It's part of being female. You've got a lot to learn, my boy."

At last, Christine went off to the dance with fingers crossed that there would be no air-raid sirens. I listened to a play on the radio with Mother until bedtime. She was excited about Dad coming home tomorrow, and so was I.

Ronnie came around midmorning on Sunday. He assumed I would be going to the bomb crater and wanted to know if he was stopping to dinner. His mum was at work all day. Ronnie stopping to dinner was fine with Mum, but two hours was all we could have out. If we stayed any later, there'd be no dinner for either of us.

We ran up the road out onto the commons and headed for the bomb crater. It was a warm day for mid-April with a clear blue sky. The crater was beyond a row of large gorse and hawthorn bushes. We heard the noise before we saw the soldiers.

The cheek. Bloody Yanks. The Boston Tea Party all over again. They had stolen our raft. There was no point arguing with them. There were over a hundred of them, many armed with guns. That didn't stop Ronnie from trying to sell our raft to them though. He got no takers but did get some gum.

The Yanks had made another raft and strengthened ours with additional timber and bolts. The washing line binding had gone. They'd replaced our oars, made of bits of fencing panels, with folding spades. The soldiers sitting on the bank made room for us so we could watch the game.

Heading from either side of the crater on their respective rafts were eight soldiers to a raft. On impact, the soldiers piled into each other, most falling into the water. It was rough, very rough. The object of the sport was to board the other raft. Once a man fell in the water, he swam to the bank.

Marv was right up front. Two others, more or less his size, were with him. The opponent's raft had no midgets either. Clunk! Straight into each other went the frontline attack. The noise and whistling from the spectators were deafening. Serious grappling went on at the front. A smaller man on the opposite raft ran up his chums' backs and took a leap into the air, hoping to land on Marv's raft. Marv's hand went up, caught him midair, and tossed him into the water. Four men were left grappling with each other. One raft heaved over, and the four went into the water.

"All bets off!" came a shout. "Time out!"

Ronnie and I watched different teams compete before we left for dinner and Dad's homecoming.

Christine was gone when we got home. "Out for the day," Mum said. "Whoever he is, Christine is smitten with him. He picked her up in his jeep an hour ago. Seems like a nice boy. He brought me these." She held up a pair of stockings. "Nylons!"

Ronnie left straight after dinner; sure he could get a trade on the raft. I washed and changed before Mum allowed me to sit out on the front-garden wall and wait for Dad. He arrived midafternoon. I saw him through the windscreen before the lorry pulled up. I hopped down and waited at the lorry door before Dad got out with his kit bag. I leapt onto him and clutched firmly around his neck. He swung me around before he put me down.

"Whoa! Whoa!" he said. "You are getting far too big for that." His beaming face was deeply tanned, highlighting his deep blue eyes. Before he could say more, Mother appeared. They kissed and hugged.

The lorry driver interrupted, coughing first and then asking, "Is it all right to go now, sir?"

Dad thanked him and said good-bye. With his kit bag on his shoulder and Mother on his arm, they went inside. I followed behind. Dad couldn't get over how much I'd grown. I was, according to him, turning into a fine young man. Mum and Dad talked for hours over cups of tea.

Dad had gone through Sicily and then into Italy from North Africa. When I asked for details, he said, "Sicily was tough. The Germans were well dug in. We had to fight every inch of the way." He was surprised how mountainous Italy was. He thought it would be slow progress pushing the Germans out of Italy, taking on one mountainous fortification after another. "One big push is all we need," he said as he summed up what was going to happen. "Then we'll be home and dry."

He looked fit and healthy, much better than when I'd seen him in Wales. He and I wrestled on the lawn while Mother prepared tea. She opened a tin of pears she'd hidden away from me. She also put a bottle of wine—real wine with a French label—on the table.

After tea, Dad and Mum and I walked over the commons down to the Cricketeer Pub. "It doesn't matter if it's not open," Dad said. "It's a fine evening for a walk. Need to stretch my legs."

Sixty or seventy American soldiers were at the Cricketeer, including Marv, Ed, and Mitch. Marv called to me, "Hi, youngster." He put his hand out to Dad. The Americans had pitchers of beer—there was only one type on sale—on long tables in the pub's front garden. We joined Marv and his companions.

"Here's to warm beer" was the toast. "Better than naught."

The Americans recognized Dad's campaign ribbons—he had two rows. Ed and Mitch had been in North Africa, but not in the same places. They swapped stories. Dad was glad they were on board at last, as he put it. Everyone seemed keen to push on with the war and get it over. There was no doubt in anyone's mind who was going to win.

Marv told Dad about Kelly in the bush. Ronnie's name came up in the conversation too. He had managed to swap the raft for a webbing belt, a large tin of ice cream, and a small pair of army boots. "Sold us our own oil drums back," Marv said. He was obviously taken with Ronnie. "He even retained the right to use the raft."

A jeep drew up, followed by shouting from our table. It was Joe. Christine was with him. They'd been to Box Hill, a beauty spot some distance away. They'd walked all the way to the top and down again. Joe got on well with Dad.

The pub had my favorite drink: Tizer, a deep orange lemonade that was much better than regular lemonade. I drank four glasses.

Joe drove us all home across the common and came in to wait for Christine to change. She was on night duty. They left with her bicycle in the back of the jeep. Mum and Dad agreed they were a fine couple.

The next week was a busy one with school in the morning and helping Dad in the garden afternoons. He dug it up from top to bottom, planting potatoes with cabbages in between. While we dug, Dad met Chalky, who was working on his allotment. They got on well. Mother had told Dad how helpful Chalky had been. We invited him for Sunday dinner. He or Dad managed to get beef.

Since he'd been home, Dad was unusually quiet. He preferred to sit with Mum in the evenings or listen to the radio. Occasionally, they went out for a walk.

One Saturday Dad took Ronnie and me fishing. We walked about a mile to the end of the cleared fields where two small lakes nestled in the woods. "They're called dew ponds," Dad said. "Formed by damning the water runoff from the common."

Between the lakes and the common was a marsh. On one side of the top lake was a sloping grass glade planted out with apple trees. The glade sloped down to the lake, giving a natural bathing area. Except for us, the lakes were deserted.

Dad spent all day spinning for pike. Eventually, he caught a small one about two feet long. It had mean eyes and rows of evil sharp teeth. Dad was pleased with his catch but returned it to the water just before we left. Ronnie and I caught a few perch and dace before we grew tired of fishing and decided to amuse ourselves on the perimeter of the swampland with our catapults. A six-foot-long grass snake startled us. Dad didn't believe us, but it was that long. We nearly trod on it before it sped off, gliding up and down the bent-over reeds.

Dad said, "You should have caught it. Best live bait you can have." He seemed relaxed. He reminded me of GranDad who was always ready with a quip.

When we got home, we found GranDad, comfortable in one of the armchairs. He looked tired, worn, and much thinner. "Fought four years in the First World War, so your grandma would be safe," he said. "A bloody war. And then the bastards came back. Don't make sense."

Mum and Dad let him carry on for a while. "Let him get it out. It'll do him good. There's no bringing Grandmother back."

Gradually, GranDad became his genial self, especially after Mother produced a half bottle of whiskey she'd won in a raffle at work. She'd been saving it for such an occasion.

Besides searchlight duty, GranDad had been working on a stretcher party with the ambulance brigade. "Terrible sights," he said, shaking his head, but he didn't elaborate. He told one amusing and touching tale that had happened a few weeks before. "Been at it all day," he said. "In and out the houses with stretchers. My overalls and helmet were covered with dust. I was coming out of the doorway backwards onto the road. Twelve or more houses were down, and I was walking on rubble." He stopped and sipped his whiskey before continuing.

"I banged into someone and shouted, 'Out of the frigging way! Emergency care!' I continued on backwards, but the chap didn't move.

Without looking, I gave the guy two or three quick four-letter words, putting off at the end of each."

Dad nodded and smiled.

GranDad started laughing. "Could have got locked up in the bloody tower, the Tower of London. It was a tall fellow in a posh suit wearing a bowler hat. Don't see much of that in London these days."

"Well?" Mother urged him on.

"Ah yes," he said. "Just behind him was a small party. Heading the party was . . ."—he paused and we waited—"our king and queen, King George VI and Queen Elizabeth. They were doing one of their tours of the bombed-out areas. Bless them. Haven't moved out of London, you know. They've taken the blitz with the rest of us." GranDad smiled. "This will make you laugh. Me and my mate got to the centre of the road, put the stretcher down, took off our tin hats, and saluted." The king came over and shook our hands, taking no notice of the dirt.

"The king told us we were doing a good job and to keep up the fine work. Then the king and queen had a word of comfort for the lady on the stretcher. Me and my mate had forgotten about her." GranDad got us laughing over this and other stories he told through the evening.

Sunday lunch was amazing. Mother did us proud. Ronnie came, and with Chalky and his wife, the table was a bit crowded. Ronnie and I sat on cabbage boxes perched on cushions. There was Tizer on the table, and Chalky brought three bottles of wine. Christine was out "a-courtin'" as Mum put it.

We had roast beef—the first I'd seen since Wales—Yorkshire pudding, mashed potatoes, brussels sprouts, dried peas soaked overnight, carrots, and swede done with cream, topped off with thick brown gravy. GranDad approved. He joked that he was thinking of staying for a year or two.

Into the third bottle of wine, GranDad and Chalky told stories of the First World War. Both GranDad and Chalky had been at the Somme, "The graveyard of tens of thousands of soldiers," GranDad said.

"Must not have recognized you because of the mud," Chalky joked.

GranDad told about a soccer match on Christmas Day in 1916. The war stopped for a day, and the English soldiers played the Germans at soccer. Chalky scored two goals and would have had more if not for the German goalkeeper. Chalky got his own back though. "I caught him squatting in a trench two days later," he said.

"And?" GranDad asked.

"Gave him six inches of cold steel."

"You what?" GranDad said, feigning disgust and adding, "You bayoneted a chap squatting? Typical guards."

"What would you expect me to do?" Chalky said, pretending to be offended. "He was reaching for his rifle."

"Expected you to offer him toilet paper," GranDad said, slapping Chalky on the back.

Morbid curiosity overcame me, and I couldn't keep my thoughts in my head. Chalky had killed a man, perhaps many. So had GranDad. It hadn't yet penetrated my head to include Dad. Hearing Chalky and GranDad telling stories made the deaths so personal, so different from hearing about them on the radio or reading the newspapers. GranDad and Chalky looked like they wouldn't hurt a fly.

I wondered what it was like to kill a man. How did Chalky feel about it? I blurted out, "What did you feel? Did you feel sorry for him?" I could have saved my breath; there wasn't going to be a philosophical discussion.

Chalky hesitated. The room went still, waiting for his answer. He looked serious as he said, "I'll tell you, John. My only thought was that I hoped they wouldn't get as good a goalkeeper next Christmas. He stopped me getting a hat trick, scoring three goals!" He gave me a wicked grin, and GranDad slapped him on the back. GranDad and Chalky broke into a rendering of "Mud, glorious mud . . ."

Mother said, "Enough sick jokes," as she cleared the table.

Dad had been cheerful but quiet during dinner. Perhaps his thoughts were too fresh for humour. There was still a war to be finished.

Ronnie and I helped with the washing up, a directive from General Mum.

GranDad stayed a week before going back to London. He and Dad took long walks together. He was still having a hard time dealing with losing Grandmother. We all missed her, but none more than GranDad. Dad tried to help him through it.

No sirens sounded for over a week. The radio news bulletins gave us the impression the Luftwaffe had suffered such losses in the air they had given up. Their losses were coupled with nightly bombings of German airfields. We heard planes flying overhead most evenings. The bombing had stopped, but it wasn't over yet. Hitler had a nasty surprise for us later.

The next few weeks went quickly. I saw Ronnie, Kelly, and Bonker at school; and they did come around once to tea. Dad wanted to meet Kelly and Bonker. He thought the four of us were England's answer to Hitler.

Ronnie had taken to wearing a cut-down American army shirt, his pockets full of gum. His mother was seeing Marvin, whom she'd met at a dance.

Dad had orders to return to his unit by the end of the third week of May. For days, the radio news gave out reports of heavy Allied bombing of German positions in Northern France and other strategic areas.

"Softening them up," Dad said, referring to the Germans. He was convinced there was a plan to attempt a landing in France, but of course, he wasn't privy to the decisions being made higher up. "I'm there to carry out orders," he said. "Not to question them. That's a soldier's lot. Like it or lump it."

The second week in May, Mother and Dad went off to Wales for a week, planning to bring my sister back with them. I was at the mercy of Christine's cooking again. On Monday morning, the usually quiet, studious atmosphere that Big Mac instilled in us was broken by a sharp yell. A boy said he'd been stung. Ten minutes later, another boy said the same thing. I wondered if the warm weather brought out the wasps or, worse still, the warble fly that drove cows mad. But no, it was Ronnie. He had found another use for the dried peas in plentiful supply. He had a short hollow bamboo cane hidden in his closed hand and a mouthful of peas.

At the fifth or sixth yell, a boy leapt up and grabbed his ear. Big Mac's eagle eye spotted Ronnie. The game was up. He spent the next hour in the sin bin. Big Mac threatened to nail him in the corner—upside down—if there was a next time. But at the end of his punishment, that wasn't all. Big Mac put him on jankers. He had to clean out the toilets every morning for a week.

Ronnie took to cleaning toilets like a duck to water. The toilets shone. At the end of class, he didn't allow boys into the toilets. They had to go around the back of the hall and have a pee. If they wanted to use the cubicles, Ronnie made them take a brush in with them, threatening to thump them if the toilet wasn't clean when they left. He became a toilet dictator, even rationing sheets of bog paper. Extra sheets cost a farthing.

Bonker, Kelly, and I thought he'd found his vocation in life. At least, we milked the situation for all it was worth, holding our noses anytime he joined us, much to his annoyance.

The week passed easily enough. Joe came around most days at teatime and did the cooking. He brought cans of tinned chicken, fish, fruit, and something he liked but I wasn't sure of, black-eyed peas.

Friday was scorching. The temperature was in the eighties with high humidity, and there wasn't a cloud in the sky or a breath of wind. It was stifling in class, even with the windows open. Big Mac let us out early, foregoing the film show. Kelly, Bonker, and I had to wait for Ronnie to put the finishing touches to his toilets. Big Mac gave him an approving smile. Jankers was over for Ronnie. It was a relief for all of us. Going to the toilet had become a crime.

We decided to go skinny-dipping at the dewponds. We had to persuade Kelly to walk that distance, but he finally agreed.

Bonker and I were sick of Ronnie's antics at the bomb crater. More boys had returned from evacuation. Because the crater was a magnet for them on a warm day, it was crowded. The Yanks were only there for a few hours on a Sunday. The rest of the time, they had training exercises. Ronnie had insisted he retain a business interest in the rafts and tried to rent them out. He always picked the biggest boy to argue with. Some of them were at least two years older. The ensuing scraps were painful.

After my second cut lip and Bonker's black eye, we persuaded Ronnie to call a truce. He hadn't gotten away scot-free. A swollen lip, cut eyebrow, and inflamed ear gave evidence to that. Kelly had survived the skirmishes intact. With his head down, he charged and then sat on his opponent until the flare-up ended.

Ronnie finally came to his senses, but only because we were his mates—or until he could find bigger mates. He wasn't well in enough with Marvin as yet, but he was working on it.

The route to the dewponds led us through the woods past the Yanks' assault course. It was strung out over two hundred yards through the woods. Ed and Mitch were there in full camouflage dress. Their helmets, covered in green string netting, held weeds and grasses. Dozens of men were going over the course with Ed and Mitch. Others barked out orders. The soldiers were in full kit—rucksacks on, ammunition belts around their waists, and automatic assault rifles strapped to their backs. They looked hot.

As we passed by, we told Mitch where we were going. He asked for directions, planning to take his men there later to cool off. We declined his offer to have a go at the course. It was hot enough just walking.

When we reached the glade leading down to the water, we heard voices and splashing. We stopped. Under the apple tree boughs, we saw about twenty young women, some sunbathing and a few swimming. They splashed in three or four feet of water. We saw piles of corduroy breeches and the green tunic shirts of land-army girls and realized they were skinny-dipping. We watched for a while, pondering the best move. We wanted to swim, but not amongst that lot. Our modesty prevented us. We decided to watch their frolicking from a distance.

The situation must have gotten to Kelly, or his eyesight needed testing. Everything was in full view, nothing left to the imagination. Without a word, down on all fours, he went crawling out of the seclusion of the ferns at the back of the glade where we hid. He ended up behind an apple tree before the open grassed area.

His rotund rear was a tempting sight, too much for Bonker. He plucked a crab apple, a bit bigger than a mushy pea, off an overhanging branch, loaded his catapult, and took aim. Bull's eye! It didn't splat; it pinged.

"Yeee-ooow!" Kelly jerked upright, his hands clutching the ample cheeks of his backside.

Two sunbathers reached him within seconds. Two others followed. Cries of "Peeping Tom" rang out. With a girl on each arm and leg, Kelly was whisked off to the water's edge.

"They're going to throw him in," Bonker said.

"Off! Off! Off!" the girls chanted. They took off Kelly's shirt. He'd already lost his cap. They unlaced his boots. He struggled. He wasn't winning. Were his trousers next?

Bonker left first, a split-second before Ronnie and me. We raced to the water's edge. Ronnie and I went one way; Bonker the other. We took out the two girls by their legs and tried to drag Kelly up by his arms. Exhausted from struggling, he couldn't help. Two girls grabbed hold of Bonker, and a third joined them.

Whoosh! Over I went. Other girls joined in the fray. In no time, I was three feet in the air, minus my clothes, heading for the water. The water was so cold it took my breath away. I surfaced to see Bonker going past me. Kelly and Ronnie were already in the water. What a sight the four of us must have made, standing with water up to our thighs, our hands firmly clutched over our John Thomases. The girls laughed at us as they splashed us. We forgot about modesty. We splashed back, working our way back to the bank. The girls didn't attempt to stop us as we ran up the bank, grabbed up our clothes, and ran up the glade to the far trees. Shouts of laughter followed us.

Where was Kelly? He hadn't run with us. We looked back. He was sauntering out of the water. He climbed up the bank, picked up his clothes, and arranged them in a neat pile. Then he went over to one of the girls' pile of clothes and picked up a green towel. He leisurely dried himself, putting the towel across his shoulders and doing a shimmy. It was a frightful sight.

Fully dressed, he doffed his cap, bowed to the girls, and walked up to meet us. The girls gave him a wild clapping and shouted, "Encore!"

Kelly grinned from ear to ear. He had forgotten about the crab apple hitting his backside. He waved and blew kisses to the girls. They waved and went back to splashing.

We dried ourselves with our shirts and left the glade by the path. Our shirts flapped over our backs, drying in the sun. We'd gone about ten yards when a bush moved. Then another bush moved. There was no breeze. The moving bushes turned into Ed and Mitch covered in ferns and grass. Having arrived a few minutes before, they were just in time to see the tail end of our escapade. We felt embarrassed. Ed and Mitch thought it huge fun and offered us a bit more fun if we wanted to stay. We did, so we promised to be quiet.

About seventy men, all camouflaged, spread out and stalked silently through the woods. Some climbed into the trees. Ed and Mitch disappeared. We climbed up a young oak. From our perch, we could see the glade clearly.

Ronnie was the first to see what was going on. Two mounds of grass moved toward the bank. The mounds moved from one clothes pile to the next. We watched the slow movement of the mounds. Eventually, the mounds turned and came back up the glade. When the mounds stood up, it was Ed and Mitch.

Whistling broke out all around the glade. The land-army girls panicked and ran for their clothes and towels. Too late. The clothes took off up the glade as if by magic. They ended up strung in the apple trees. Some girls took to the water, while others ran to the trees. They had one hand on their crotches, the other across their chests.

All went quiet. I saw movement in the ferns below the oak tree. Shouting broke out. In the far corner of the glade, seventy men or more, four abreast, ran in formation, chanting as they ran. Mitch was in front, Ed in the rear. Their chant was

> Such lovely boobs!
> Mustn't look. Mustn't touch.
> Could get us in the news.

They pretended not to look, hands shading their eyes as they passed the girls. The girls shrieked.

As the platoon headed out toward the other side of the glade, the chanting faded away. It was time for us to disappear as well.

On the way home, we saw that some army tents had been removed and others were coming down. We stopped to talk to the soldiers.

Was it my imagination? I asked Ronnie and Bonker if they heard what I heard. They stopped talking and listened for several minutes and finally nodded in agreement.

After his experience, Kelly wasn't stuttering—there were a few pauses, an "err" and "arr"; but other than that, he was quite lucid and replied quickly to questions. For a change, Kelly was telling the stories. Lewd stories of his fantasies with nude land-army girls kept us in fits of laughter.

He hadn't forgotten about being stung with a crab apple, though, and his graphic explanation of what he was going to do with a block and tackle over a tree bough made us wince. Bonker's manhood was under threat. Amid hysterics, he pleaded with Kelly to string him up by the neck instead. Kelly was having none of it. He enjoyed expressing his thoughts, however obscene.

A jeep was parked outside when I got home. I figured it was Joe's. He'd spent his free time at the house since Mum and Dad had been away. I was doing very well out of it. Joe would slip me a sixpence or a shilling and suggest, with a wink, that I get lost for an hour or two.

I found my dinner—plenty of chicken and lightly browned sliced potatoes—in the oven, set on warm. I wasn't sure about the black-eyed peas. "They're an acquired taste," Joe had said. I wondered how long it took to acquire a taste for them. Joe had also left two slices of bread spread with a treat, peanut butter. That I liked. I sat at the kitchen table and tucked into my dinner. The day's events left me ravenous. After another two slices of bread and peanut butter, I felt human again.

Voices came from the front room. When I first came in, I called out that I was home, but no one replied. I opened the kitchen door and walked down the passageway to the front room, a room we used only when we had visitors since it was the only room with decent furniture. The door was closed, but it usually was. I was only allowed in on special occasions and after a bath and change of clothes. I shouted through the door that I was home.

"Come in," Joe called.

He sat on the settee, dressed in an army T-shirt and a pair of shorts. Christine sat in an armchair, wearing an overlarge army T-shirt. She didn't look happy. Her eyes were red. She'd been crying.

"All right?" I asked.

Christine nodded.

"I'm leaving in the morning," Joe said.

"Going away for good," Christine said and broke into a sob.

"It's not for good," Joe said. "I'll be back."

"Promise," Christine said.

Joe promised.

"Where are you going?" I asked.

"He won't tell me," Christine blurted out.

"That ain't fair," Joe said. "You know I can't. Even if I was sure."

"You'll look after yourself? You'll write. You'll come back?" Christine went on and on.

"Sure. How many times do I have to promise?"

"You do love me? We will marry? I'll wait," she said.

It was time for me to get lost. I didn't need persuading. "Sorry, can't stop," I said. "Ronnie's waiting for me. Be around Ronnie's 'til late. Leave the key under the mat." I wished Joe luck.

He stood up and shook my hand, wished me all the best, and said he was sure I'd do fine.

I waved to Christine, who didn't respond. I met Ronnie coming down the road, hands in his pockets, whistling to himself. I told him about Christine crying and Joe leaving.

He said his mother had been crying too. "Mum's getting stupid over Marvin leaving," he said.

"Will you miss him?" I asked.

Ronnie was thoughtful, most unusual for him. "You know, I really like that guy. So does Mum. Yes, I'll miss him. I hope he comes back, for Mum's sake. She's been lonely since she lost Dad. I've not see her so happy since Marvin's been around."

Mum and Dad returned the next day, bringing my sister with them. She had grown, but nothing like I had. There was a good six inches between us. Dad had already given her the nickname of Tich, a name that stuck. After four years, we were finally a family again, but only for two days. Dad had to return to the barracks.

His departure really hit me. My stomach turned over with a queasy feeling, a gnawing sickness. Mum, my sister, and even Christine cried. Dad had been quiet, but I was going to miss him. He left emptiness in the house that only he could fill.

The night he left, I did something I hadn't done for months. I prayed for the safety of Dad, Joe, Marvin, Ed, and Mitch. I should have included us all. I was under the mistaken impression we were safe, a grave error.

Chapter 10

LASTING MEMORIES

The departures of Dad and the Yanks left a big hole. It was back to the daily grind of school and homework.

There was no money and little to spend it on even if we had some. Strolling across the common with our catapults, shooting at anything that moved became monotonous. To make matters worse, the good weather of May ended in a thunderstorm. A southwesterly had blown in, giving a wet start to June.

The winds were fierce, breaking boughs off trees. Rain lashed at us as Ronnie and I walked across the common to school. Hand-me-down raincoats had dried up, and we used clothes rations sparingly. A new raincoat grabbed too many clothing coupons, even if Mother could have found one to buy, so our rain gear consisted of a camouflaged ground sheet with a slit cut in the center. This, coupled with a wide-brimmed sou'wester, kept most of the rain out. Ronnie and I arrived at school feeling damp. Bonker had made it on his own. Kelly had a cold.

Big Mac beamed. It made us nervous. Either something personal had happened or he was going to give us a test. He had a knack for testing us at our limit of knowledge, usually a prelude to a new set of exercises or setting some of us extra homework.

He had drawn a map on the blackboard, a part of France, the English Channel, and a section of the south coast of England.

Good lord, I thought. We're going to have a geography test.

Before he spoke, I could hear it coming. "Copy the maps from the board. Put in the towns or features as they are called." There were usually twenty questions, and we got extra homework for missing more than five.

"What do you know about France?" Ronnie whispered, ready to copy. It was easier to let him copy than to help him out with his extra homework.

"A bit," I said. "Frenchmen live there."

He punched my shoulder. "Dickhead."

"No talking in back" came Big Mac's deep Scottish brogue. He stared at us over his spectacles, still smiling. This was getting creepy.

Class started with the Lord's Prayer, a prayer for king and country, a prayer for all our servicemen, and Ronnie's just audible prayer for the sirens to go off so lessons would finish with a trip to the air-raid shelter.

The test was to begin, or so we thought, but Big Mac liked surprising us. We never knew what he knew for sure or what he ignored, but he didn't miss much. The day before, right out of the blue, he said, "John, stand up and spell Frisian, the animal, and freesia, the flower." Afterward, I checked and found I'd used the words incorrectly in last week's composition and wondered how he'd remembered. At least, I knew it wasn't just with me; it was with all of us.

"We are back," began Big Mac. "We are back in France. The D-day invasion has started."

"What the hell is he on about?" Ronnie whispered.

I wasn't sure either. We'd been bombing German bases in France for weeks. It was on the news most nights.

Mac explained. The invasion started in the early hours with a huge paratrooper drop behind the coastal defenses. Assault troops hit the beaches at first light. Massive air and naval bombardment supported the ground troops. The day was the sixth of June 1944, D-day. To us, the day was nothing special, just wet and windy.

Big Mac had told us about the evacuation of Dunkirk in June 1940, described by Winston Churchill as "our darkest hour." A Canadian division tried to secure a beachhead last year, suffering appalling casualties. Now we were going back. At least, our forces were invading. We'd have to wait for the outcome.

Big Mac's map board showed the location of the beach assault. The landing site was a good 150 miles down the French coast from Dunkirk in a sweeping bay, the Bay of the Seine. The D-day invasion began on the Normandy beaches.

Through the next week, Big Mac added to the map, giving figures and his own commentary. He brought a radio into the classroom, and we listened to the hourly news bulletins. Normal lessons went by the way.

Our initial surprise turned from a grudging interest into keen excitement. On the third day, the radio reported that British and Canadian forces repelled a German counterattack near Caen. The Allied line held. We had a firm toehold in France.

Ronnie jumped up on his chair, arms out, rat-a-tatting and machine-gunning the four rows of boys in front. Luckily, Big Mac was in good humour. He told Ronnie to sit down, waiving the usual hour in the sin bin. Our excitement was contained by conscious worry. Many boys had dads in the armed forces. None of us knew where they were or how they were faring.

The worry at home was more intense. Christine and Mother, through the phone at work, tried to get information, but the only news they had was that the names they gave weren't on the casualty lists. Neither Mother nor Christine could find out the whereabouts of Dad or Joe. That was classified information.

Anxiety and worry showed in their faces. There was no laughter in the house. Mother was very edgy. The slightest misdeed got the whiplash of her tongue. I kept out of the way, either going out with the lads or playing cricket with other boys who had returned from evacuation. At night, I lay on my mattress under the stairs—my sister had taken my room—reading with a torch.

At the end of the first week of the D-day invasion, the Allied Forces secured a beachhead seventy miles wide and penetrated thirty miles inland. Reinforcements poured in. The push into mainland Europe and Germany was underway. Casualty figures were being released from the D-day invasion, a frightening estimate of over seven thousand men dead, missing, or wounded. The American forces on the beach section, code-named Omaha, had met stiff opposition. Many never even saw a German, never fired a shot. Over three thousand soldiers were feared lost. A newspaper carried the headline: "Bloody Omaha," with a report of the landing. Everything that could go wrong did. The air strike intended to eliminate the German defense positions had missed the target. A tough, experienced German division had arrived and was already firmly entrenched. Many amphibious tanks sank in the rough sea. The forces finally secured the beachhead with a combination of frontal assault, a pincher movement of ground troops and heavy shelling of German defense positions by naval destroyers, but at an appalling loss of life to both sides.

Over the next week, the toehold in France grew stronger. The Allied armies built up for the breakout from Normandy and the liberation of France.

At home, another worrying time was on the horizon. It would be some time before we could sleep safely in our beds. It was too early to be complacent, far too early.

In the third week of June, the weather brightened. The euphoria of the invasion subsided. Except for an update on positions and Big Mac's interpretation, lessons continued as normal. He reverted to his artful ways. The sin bin came back into use, along with toilet cleaning. Kelly got several doses of both.

Now that his stuttering had disappeared, he wouldn't stop talking. Big Mac became exasperated with him—a blessing since it took the heat off the rest of us. We had long since worked out that if there was no toilet cleaner, Big Mac had to do it himself.

After school, we waited for Kelly to finish his jankers, holding our noses when he joined us. He had managed to get a reel of cotton, so we were going newting. Kelly had seen crested newts in the tank traps near the cricket field.

The traps had become a haven for wildlife, including reeds, bull rushes, lilies, ducks, moorhens, and coots. Frogs, sticklebacks, and other small fish populated the water. Nestled in the reed was the tiny nest of the reed warbler. Judging by her activity, she was on her second brood. Dragonflies zigzagged across the water, skimming above the surface. Their blue fluorescent wings shimmered in the sun. The tank trap, built for war, harboured so much peace.

Resting on the dyke's bottom were large great-crested newts, eight-inch dragons, black on top with large comb crests. Their undersides were a mottle of white, yellow, and brown. For us lads, newt fishing was a pleasant way of passing time. There wasn't much involved. We tied a small pebble and worm on the end of a length of cotton. We prowled along the edge of the tank trap until we spotted a newt. Plop! In went the pebble, settling down near the newt. It never failed. The newt had the worm in seconds. Up came the pebble, worm, and newt.

After a couple of lazy hours, we'd caught fifteen and held them in a rusty old tin. Kelly caught a whopper, twelve inches long. Eventually, though, we got bored and returned the newts to the water. Ronnie suggested we walk up to where the Yanks had camped to see if they'd left anything useful.

On our way, we passed a ditched greenfield, home to fifty or more geese. I decided to show off my farm prowess by walking through a gaggle. A few large ganders decided I was easy prey and ran full tilt at me, necks stretched out, hissing. I just made it over the ditch before my backside got a serious pecking, much to everyone's amusement, except mine, of course.

We passed a block of cottages to our left, the last houses before the common. The first cottage had a grapevine covered with white unripe grapes growing against the wall. In a couple months' time, they would be easy pickings. We made note of our find: over the low wooden fence, a few strides down the lawn, a hop down the retaining wall onto the path, and bingo, we'd have ourselves some grapes. Turned out we visited the grapevine sooner than we'd planned.

"Not seen one of them," I said, pointing to the sky. Traveling toward us no more than 1,500 feet above ground level was a black torpedo-shaped body with short midcentre wings. The engine appeared to be mounted over the rear end of the fuselage, a long tube emitting flames. The plane—at least, we assumed it was a plane—emitted a loud thrumming sound, a resonant throbbing. Thrumm. Thrumm. Thrumm.

We hopped over the ditch and stood on the bank to get a better view. As it got nearer, the thrumming ceased. The nose dropped. It was coming down, coming down fast.

I yelled, "It's coming straight at us!"

The air filled with the sound of air-raid sirens alternating through several octaves: the warning signal, the first we'd heard for nearly three months.

I took off across the road, hurdling the small wooden fence, flew over the lawn, and threw myself down on the path against the cottage wall. Ronnie and Bonker followed me.

I heard a sickening thud—whoooom!—and a deafening explosion. The ground shifted under me. The vibration lifted me off the ground. Dirt battered the grapevine-covered wall and rained down on us. A dull pain hit both my eardrums. I clamped my hands over my ears.

We lay still for a couple of minutes before Bonker got up. Ronnie and I got to our knees, pushed our fingers in and out of our ears, trying to cure the ringing. My hearing returned to near normal, but my eardrums still ached. We brushed ourselves down with our hands.

"What in Jesus's name was that?" Bonker asked.

"Don't know," Ronnie said. "Whatever it was, you can have my share."

"Trust you," Bonker said. "You never give anything away that's useful."

"Where's Kelly?" I asked, looking around.

We ran up the lawn and jumped over the fence onto the pavement. Turning around, I saw that most of the cottages had lost their windows and roof tiles. The road was strewn with debris, mainly dirt and small stones with the odd larger stone and wad of earth.

Smoke rose up to our left over the brow of the gorse land. Whatever it was had landed about three hundred yards away. Thick black smoke rose into the sky, and the smell of pungent, acrid sulphurous fumes mingled in the light breeze.

"Kelly! Kelly!" we shouted.

There was no reply.

We looked up and down the road.

"Kelly! Kelly!" We started to panic.

At last, a muddy cap followed by an even muddier face appeared out of the ditch. One arm rose, then another. Kelly stood up. He was plastered in mud. Shaken up as we were, we couldn't stifle a laugh. Poor Kelly! He usually got the sticky end. We ran over to help him out of the ditch.

It had muddy water at the bottom, and Kelly had flattened himself facedown in it. We started to pull him out by his arms. Bonker pulled me across and changed sides with me. Kelly was plastered elsewhere, and I was downwind.

"Mary mother of Jesus!" Kelly said, using one of his mother's expressions. "What in hell was that, John?"

I shook my head. "Don't know, Kelly. I hope it's one of ours gone astray and not one of theirs." After thinking about it, I added, "It must be one of ours. We control the sky now. No German bombers can get through." I believed this to be true. Big Mac believed it. Little did we know the Germans were going to launch over nine thousand of the blighters at us.

We jumped up the bank and tore up bundles of dried grass to give Kelly a hand in cleaning himself. He dropped his trousers, intending to clean up the mess not caused by the muddy water. We made him pull them up and sent him off through the long grass to the privacy of a gorse bush. A bomb we could take; Kelly's backside we couldn't.

Sitting on the side of the bank, I felt my knees trembling. I put my hands out flat in front of me. They shook too. I felt nervous inside. All confidence had left me. "Bonker, how do you feel?" I asked.

"Not too good," he said. "I felt all right until I saw Kelly's arse."

"You looked?"

"Couldn't help it," he said. "He dropped his trousers in front of me. It was two feet away, give or take an inch."

"Ugh," I said, lying back on the bank. I started laughing. Ronnie and Bonker laughed too.

"Two feet away," I repeated. "Ugh! Ugh!"

Bonker shook with laughter. I felt the tension flowing out as we all laughed at Bonker's ghastly experience.

When Kelly returned, he still stank. "Kelly," I said. "I think you need to go home."

"Why?" He had a blank expression.

We held our noses. He finally got the message.

The all clear siren went off.

"I hope they've got it right this time," Ronnie said. "I don't want another surprise like that."

We all nodded.

"If that bomb was one of ours, why the siren?" he asked.

"It must have been ours," Bonker insisted.

We sat and watched Kelly waddle up the road. He didn't have far to go. We waved good-bye and set off through the long grass and gorse bushes to inspect the bomb crater.

From the path alongside the common, we saw where it landed. Two hundred and fifty yards away was a huge mound of earth, emitting a plume of thick black smoke as if the mound were on fire. A thick canopy of sulphurous haze engulfed us, the fumes catching in the back of our throats and smarting our eyes. The bomb landed in the area where the Americans had their base. If they hadn't moved on, the war would have ended there for most of them.

A second or two earlier would have meant the end of us too. We were mindful of this and thoughtful of the near miss. It was strange. Someone had chucked a bomb at us, and we were in high spirits, not dismal about the bomb but uplifted that it missed us. We decided not to go any nearer the crater. The next day maybe, when things cooled down.

Ronnie was the first to notice the pram.

"Where?" we asked.

He pointed. "There in the gorse bush."

Fifty yards farther down the path, there was a pram stuck halfway up in a large gorse bush. We sprinted down the path. Off to one side of the pram was a shawl-wrapped bundle. It was a crying baby.

Then we saw the mother. She must have bounced off the bush and traveled on, ending up in the long grass. Her body lay slightly twisted, legs splayed out. Her face twisted to one side, with one hand above her head. The other arm lay trapped beneath her body.

Bonker and I waded into the gorse bush, oblivious to the hostile spikes. While he pulled the pram out, I got the baby out of the tangle of clawing needles. Ronnie went over to check the lady but quickly came back. "I think she's dead," he said. "She ain't moving."

I dumped the whimpering baby into the pram and went nearer to where she lay. Bonker and Ronnie stood a couple of paces back. I'd handled dead calves and pigs, but I'd never actually touched a dead person.

I didn't feel fear. Instead, I felt concern and worry and wondered what I should do. Big Mac's first aid lesson words came back to me loud and clear: "Don't move them. Keep them warm. Get help."

"Bonker, make the baby comfortable," I ordered.

For some reason, Bonker and Ronnie instinctively turned to me. I approached the mother. She was young, probably nineteen or twenty, certainly younger than Christine. I'd seen her pushing the pram around the estate. Her thin blue cotton dress was torn, her dress indecently high. I bent and pulled her dress down and knelt to look at her face. I slipped my hand through the grass and moved her head slightly. Her face was lightly grazed with a shimmer of blood. Her eyes were open, the pupils high in her head. I put my middle finger and forefinger on her neck, the way I'd been taught, to feel for a pulse but couldn't feel one. My own heart pounded. The side of her face twitched; her eyelashes flickered.

"She could be alive!" I yelled. "Ronnie, run to the cottages and get a blanket. Break in if you have to. Be quick."

Ronnie took off like a hare.

"Bonker, stay here and look after the baby and keep an eye on the mother. I'm going for help." I ran down the path. Chalky lived in a cottage not far away. Getting his help was the only clear thought in my head. He'd know what to do. He carried a first aid kit with him in a satchel strapped to his bicycle.

He stood outside his cottage, surveying the bomb damage. Most of his windows had blown out. I gasped out what information I had.

"Baby and mother?" Chalky repeated. "Is mother alive? Exactly where?" Satisfied he had the correct details, he used the walkie-talkie field telephone he carried, requested an ambulance, and gave directions. He hopped on his bike and cycled away toward the common.

I leaned against the cottage wall. My lungs felt like they were bursting. My mouth tasted of sulphur. My side ached from a stitch. I trembled. The last hour's events had caught up with me. It took me ten minutes or more to recover.

An ambulance passed as I walked back up to the common. After it passed, I broke into a jog. I knew there was nothing more I could do, so I don't know why I hurried. Eventually, I tired and settled to a slow walk. My thoughts focused on the young mother. I willed myself into thinking she would be all right.

When the ambulance returned from the common, I waved, wanting them to stop and tell me how she was, but it rushed past with the siren going.

Chalky wasn't far behind on his bicycle. He greeted me with good news. She was alive, but she probably had a broken arm and a concussion. "She and her baby were lucky you boys found her," Chalky said, and I felt joy sweep over me. "Not many people out with the sirens going and a bomb going off. Lucky to get an ambulance. Another bomb dropped in town. Five minutes later, and you would have missed me. Two babies on the way on my patch. What a day to be born."

He told me the bomb was German. The radio called them unmanned flying bombs. Several hit the London area that morning. Everyone was on alert because more were expected. Chalky had sent Bonker and Ronnie home. He said I should go home too.

Just before I reached the estate, the warning sirens went off again. I sprinted for the public air-raid shelter, joining a dozen others inside, and sat on the first available bunk. As the siren died down, we heard the thrumming of another flying bomb. We listened in silence as it passed overhead. The noise faded and then stopped abruptly, followed seconds later by a muffled explosion. Three more flying bombs passed nearby in the next two hours. I sat in the shelter for another hour after that. Although no all clear siren sounded, people decided to risk making for home. I did too.

On the way home, another flying bomb passed in the distance. I couldn't see it, but the sound got to me. I arrived home, breathless from running, and found Christine and my sister under the Morrison table. Mother wasn't home from work yet. She didn't get back until after nine. Three worried people greeted her. She had waited hours for the all clear signal, but it never came; so she, too, chanced coming home during a quiet period. She persuaded Christine to stay home from work that night. Christine didn't need much persuasion.

A few minutes later, we heard the drone of yet another flying bomb. My sister joined me at the other end of the mattress under the stairs. Christine and Mother stayed under the Morrison table. I doubt anyone slept long. One after another, flying bombs passed overhead through the night. The wailing of the air-raid sirens kept us awake.

The next morning's news gave details of the flying bomb. Coded the V1, it traveled at four hundred miles per hour, making it difficult to stop. The unmanned rocket planes were likely launched from bases in Northern France. "Every effort is being made to stop them," the announcer said. Over two hundred and forty landed in the London area in the last twenty-four hours. People were warned to be on constant alert and not to risk unnecessary traveling.

The blitz attack of V1s went on for another three months amid the constant wail of sirens. Through the day and night, I cringed as the thrumming noise came nearer and nearer. Waiting for the rocket motor to cut out, followed by an eerie silence wore on my nerves. During that silence came the awareness that someone, somewhere, would probably die in the next few seconds. Then the explosion came and with it the worry. Had a man, woman, child, or a whole family died? The estimate for deaths and casualties exceeded those of the 1940 London blitz.

Several nights, neither Mother nor Christine made it home. My sister stayed with friends. I'd lie awake under the stairs alone, listening, holding my breath as the doodlebug motors cut out. Eventually, fatigue overcame me; and I sank into a fitful sleep, waking as planes droned overhead or explosions boomed in the distance.

The erratic nature of the doodlebug meant the suburban boroughs south of London took the brunt of the bombing. We were on the inner fringe, so danger was always with us. We were always on guard. We played musical chairs with air-raid shelters, traveling during quiet times but always mindful of where to find the next shelter. We strained our ears, listening for the thrumming and combing the skies for a rocket burbling its way to death and destruction. In true Hitlerian style, the bombs weren't made for victory but for vengeance.

In early September, the rapid advance of our Allied armies eastward through France reached the launch sites of the V1s, ending their reign. However, it was only a short respite from something worse, much bigger, and more deadly.

Blaring sirens woke me. Mother hurried my sister from her bedroom to the mattresses under the stairs. No burbling. No sound. In the empty night, we first felt a thud that shook the walls. Then silence. More air-raid sirens wailed. The sirens kept up right through the night. It was going to be that way up to nearly the end of the war.

Hitler had a new more deadly rocket, the V2, a forty-foot monster. It traveled in a huge hyperbola at speeds up to four thousand miles per hour. Completing its journey from launch to destination in only three or four minutes, it was indefensible. With little respite, I was a prisoner in an air-raid shelter for the next five months, give or take a few interludes.

I went to see where the V2 had landed. It landed plumb in the middle of the American campsite, creating a huge crater sixty feet across. The earth still smoldered. I smelled that acrid sulphurous smell. Ronnie was there with a crowd of people, looking for shrapnel.

Mother didn't want any part of a bomb in the house. She said, "It's bad luck. Its brother may come looking for it."

I hadn't seen much of Ronnie through the summer. His mother, like mine, had forbidden him to roam too far. She allowed only essential journeys, and he wasn't to take too long on those.

My sister palled up with a girl down the road and spent much of her time in their outside air-raid shelter. Her mother fitted it up like a second home. I stayed by myself during interludes, weeding the potato patch or catapulting at crows that dared to land in it. It was a long, lonely summer.

I started a new school in September, a proper full-time school a mile on from the church hall. It was an hour's walk from home. Day after day, week after week, I sat in an air-raid shelter and then hurried home with air-raid sirens going full blast. Experiencing a near miss by a V2 rocket was nerve-racking, stretching every fibre. There was no warning, no air-raid siren, just a huge explosion in the distance followed by the ground shaking and a plume of rising smoke. What nerves I had left failed me. I ran in a panic the last mile home. That was the end of schooling until late spring.

Ronnie went off to stay with his uncle. Mother gave serious thought to sending my sister and me back to Wales, but we didn't want to go. I don't think she wanted us to go either. Whatever the outcome, we wanted to stay together.

The winter months were tense and gloomy with long periods of rain and huge blankets of dark clouds. It was impossible to plan a day, and a night's sleep was never guaranteed. We knew that some never woke in the morning.

However, there were bright intervals through the gloom. Letters arrived from Dad and Joe in October, four months after we'd last seen them. The letters came in two bundles, one for Mum and one for Christine, with no news of their exact whereabouts except they were somewhere in France. The letters were brief. Neither had much to say about the fighting.

In one of Joe's letters, he said that Ed and Mitch "had not made it." They tackled one too many minefields. They had both been decorated for bravery multiple times before being killed. Marvin had been injured and shipped back to England, but Joe didn't know where. Dad and Joe were concerned about us. They'd heard about the V bombs and hoped we weren't taking risks.

Then came the bombshell—different from Hitler's. Joe was concerned for Christine who was carrying their baby. That was the first I'd heard about it. Christine didn't want me to know since she wasn't married, but Joe didn't care. He'd written to Christine's parents and to his parents. He wanted her to return to the safety of Ireland.

"Oh well," Christine sighed. "Now my parents are going to find out. God only knows what they're going to say. I'd better write them too." She worried about her parents' reaction and discussed the problem at length with Mother. Mother helped Christine write a letter to them.

Just before Christmas, two letters arrived for Christine. One was from Joe's parents. They were delighted with the news. Joe was their only son, and they wanted to keep in touch with Christine, "even if, God forbid, something happened to him." They offered to help in any way and even enclosed money for her. "Look at this," Christine said. "Two month's salary. They are kind people, just like Joe."

The other letter was from Christine's parents. They wanted her to come home. Joe had asked them to persuade her to go home.

She left just after Christmas. The baby was only a few weeks away. Mother had mixed feelings about Christine leaving. She thought her leaving was best for her and the baby, but she was going to miss her. I had got used to her being around. She was like a big sister to me, so I was going to miss her too though it meant I could have my bedroom back on quiet nights.

Once she left, the atmosphere at home changed. Christine's chirpy spirit had been a foil to combat the anxiety, the melancholy that would set in, the heaviness of Mother's mind, and the apprehension she felt. Christine's sparkle had illuminated the household. Her leaving was a light going out in our lives, especially for Mother, who turned to me more and more for comfort and optimism. It wasn't a role I was equipped to deal with, never knowing quite what to say. The highlights were Dad's letters, arriving in twos or threes. They lifted Mother's spirits, even when she was really in the dumps, having a "blue day," as she put it. Besides Dad's optimistic way of writing about the future and what he was planning when the war was over, the letters meant one thing. He was still alive.

Who was in more danger was a moot point. We were all at war. We were all in the front line. Hitler's vengeance had no boundaries. More and more civilians were being killed and maimed every day.

By the end of March, the Allied forces succeeded in all but surrounding Germany. On some fronts, they penetrated into Germany. Massive air attacks and bombardment of German cities evened up the score most believed was their due. The V2 rocket launching bases were overrun, and except for the occasional rocket, the bombing ceased.

Talks of the war's end were premature though. Hitler intended to fight to the last even though his position was futile. He was going to sacrifice several more million lives in making a land stand. But his own people were the victims. The fighting was brutal.

Newspapers and radio news were full of combat stories. More onerous were the stories of the dark side of the war, the gruesome stories of the suffering, rape, mutilation and murder of civilians, and the misery inflicted on the people of the occupied countries. The fist narrative I read in the newspaper, along with photographs, was an account of the atrocities on Oradour-sur-Glane, a small country village located in east-central France. As retribution, German soldiers slaughtered over six hundred and forty civilians: farmers, merchants, housewives, schoolchildren, and babies. They bayoneted babies or crushed their skulls with rifle butts. The German soldiers set fire to the village.

It sickened me and gave me nightmares. I saw the German soldiers, their bayonets poised, and I'd wake up in a cold sweat as the bayonets were coming down.

Even more horrifying acts of barbarism unfolded as the Allied forces swept through France and on into Belgium and Holland. Daily the newspapers carried stories of the grim legacy of German occupation. The unraveling atrocities were only a foreshadowing of the stark, heinous crimes committed by the Germans. Those crimes would haunt the German nation forever.

I hadn't been sorry that school had finished in the autumn of 1944. Besides the anxiety of the V1 rocket bombings and the long daily stints in the school air-raid shelters, discipline was harsh. Teachers used the cane and slipper liberally to assure total obedience. Talking out of turn, dawdling on the way to the shelters, or worse still, picking an apple from the trees on the way to the bunkers met with retribution.

In six weeks, I had earned three wallopings across my backside, two with a slipper and one with a thin willowy cane. Six of the best hurt. I had trouble walking afterward, let alone sitting. When I mentioned the caning to Mother, she thought a bit of discipline wouldn't do me harm. "You must have deserved it," she said. "Do you good." No sympathy there.

It was with trepidation I returned to school in April. Ronnie, Bonker, and Kelly, all older, attended the senior school. I couldn't join them until after the summer. My sister was lucky. A girls' school for boarders opened in the mansion house on the estate, and Mother had been able to get her in. I still had over an hour's walk each way to school.

The headmaster of the new school was a beast of a man. His name was Rutter. We called him Rottweiler. Except for his round wire-framed spectacles, he was a Hitler clone. He was shorter, not more than six or seven inches taller than me. He parted his dark hair Hitler style with a quiff at the front and copied Hitler's dark clipped moustache. He even walked like the Hitler I'd seen in newsreels, slightly stooped, feet splayed out, hands clenched behind his back.

Rottweiler enjoyed inflicting pain. Morning assembly seldom went past without an unfortunate boy getting six of the best across his backside, preceded by a lecture on how Rottweiler would not tolerate this or that: talking in class, breaking a school window, or sobbing before the cane.

I got my first whacking after only three days for trying to set a school record by peeing up the wall of the outside toilets. I made it over the wall, a class record, much admired by my classmates, but not by the playground attendant. Unfortunately, she'd been on the other side of the wall. She caught me in my glory, leaning back, fly open, a two-handed approach, one for trajectory, the other to control the orifice. Oh, boy! She was mad. She snatched off her felt hat. The boys couldn't stop laughing.

Rottweiler was in a rage the next morning. The school wouldn't stop laughing, but he stopped them. "The next one to smirk will join me on stage," he threatened. The hall quieted. I got an extra stroke for laughing, but I didn't laugh for long. The pain was bad enough, but the deep-seated ache stayed with me for two more days.

A week into school, the teachers told us some lessons would be cancelled that morning because a medical team was coming in. I must have missed the earlier briefing. Many mothers turned up to escort their sons down the medical lines set up with desks in the hall and school passageway. It was a repetition of the evacuation medical: nit nurse, who'd have you shaved bald at the slightest sign of fleas or ringworm, eyesight check, trousers down, arses up, needle in the right arm, dentist at the end of the corridor. I wasn't looking forward to another dose of what was good for me.

No, thank you, I thought. It was a ruse. They weren't fooling me. They were checking and immunizing, so we could survive the school dinners. I handed my white card to a nurse and told her I'd been asked to give it to her because the boy was absent from school. I returned to the classroom, rather pleased with myself. I wasn't as pleased the next morning when Rottweiler gave me another six of the best.

I managed to earn two more whackings over the next three weeks. One I got for shinnying up a drainpipe to retrieve a tennis ball trapped in the gully of a hip roof. The other I got for being involved in a fight not of my making.

The school bully picked on the wrong guy. He twisted arms of younger boys and pulled their ears. He'd been trying to pick a fight with me for three weeks for no reason I could see other than I was new at the school and I existed. Finally, he lit my fuse, a very short one. I gave him a black eye and a bloody nose. I escaped relatively unscathed, which explains why I got the caning.

After that episode, boys left me alone in the playground but not in the classroom. The bully and his mates got their own back. Our class master, an ugly, sneering bull-faced man was short of breath and even shorter on temper. He ruled the class with a size 12 plimsole, a black canvas upper with an orange rubber sole. At the slightest hint of misbehaviour, Bull-face gave two, three, six whacks across the backside, depending on his mood.

The classroom felt like a morgue. The whole school was like an Indian burial ground, a place where the spirit left the body. The difference was the body was very much alive.

Bull-face prowled around the class. He was in a bad mood, and the class sensed it. There was a deadly hush. Something was wrong. Something was going to happen. We felt the tension.

"Desk lids up," he ordered.

We sat in pairs of desks with individual desk lids. I opened mine and instinctively closed it. My eyes had fixed on a size 12 plimsole. There was nowhere to put it, nowhere to hide it. There was only one thing to do: face up and explain. I stood up, plimsole in hand.

"Is this what you're looking for?" I asked.

There was a gasp and then reactive, nervous laughter. Thirty boys were relieved it wasn't them. A few in the know laughed in jest.

Bull-face ordered me to the front of the class to take another whacking. I protested and insisted I was innocent. I weighed up my chances of reaching the door before Bull-face. It wasn't far away. I had taken six of the best four days ago and the slipper yesterday for knocking over an inkwell. I'd had enough. I was determined to leave the school. What was the point? I had learnt little and was too frightened to ask questions. At that moment, fear and thoughts of survival were paramount in my brain. I was sick of being beaten.

I had rights as a human being. Even prisoners of war had the Geneva Conventions on punishment and welfare. At school, there were no clearly defined laws of conduct and no avenues of appeal. Just being alive and breathing was an excuse for a beating. I determined to make a stand. No more corporal punishment. Nobody was going to hit me again. Oh, how foolish!

"No, sir," I said with determination. "You are not going to hit me anymore. I refuse to let you. You are a bully. When my dad gets home, you are in for it." I couldn't count on Mum, but I was sure Dad would take my side.

Bull-face blew a fuse. He twitched as if his finger plugged into a light socket. His breathing got loud and even shorter. He leapt, passing between the desks, and came straight at me. He knocked over three desks. Boys who didn't move fast enough fell to the floor.

Bull-face grabbed the plimsole and then grabbed me by the collar. He dragged me, struggling, out through the door and across the hall into the headmaster's office, hitting me all the time with the slipper on the legs, back, and head.

Rottweiler held me over the desk while Bull-face hit me across the rump and back with a willowy cane. I struggled in vain. I'd had about twelve whacks before they let me go. That was their mistake. I was past being hurt. Somewhere between not feeling any pain and fainting, anger boiled inside me. I kicked them both before I reached the door. I ran out through the hall, through the cloakroom and across the playground, clearing with an Olympic one-hand assisted leap the row of railings that had escaped salvage. The headmaster caught up with me halfway across the playground. He got in three or four whacks across my shoulders and head before I broke for the safety of the pavement outside the school.

I heard someone shouting, "Stop that! Stop that!" from across the road.

I ran for over a mile, looking back only to make sure no one followed. It was only after I slowed down that I realized how much I hurt. My legs, backside, back, and head throbbed. My body burned. I put my hand underneath my shirt and found a particularly sore area. Blood covered my hand when I withdrew it.

Just then, the air-raid siren sounded off, the first for three weeks. I ignored it. I heard the muffled explosion of a bomb in the distance, but I didn't care. I was angry, angry at the world, angry at Hitler, angry at being beaten, angry at injustice. My anger was cold, a chilling fury. At that moment, I could have killed, killed in cold blood. I understood where Chalky and GranDad had been in the First World War. I understood where Dad was now. I was past fear. If I had the means, I would have returned and killed Bull-face and Rottweiler.

That evening, Mother examined my wounds. I couldn't hide the pain. I looked over my shoulder into a long mirror in the bathroom. I had cuts in several places. Black-and-blue weals crisscrossed down my body. A scab was forming over the cut on the back of my head. Mother questioned me and wrote down what I said and then checked it with me again. I told no lies. I didn't have to. She dressed the open wounds with ointment. I went to bed early but couldn't find a comfortable position to sleep in.

The next day, I was so stiff I could hardly move. It was another three days before I could walk normally. In the afternoon, Mother brought a school inspector, dressed smartly in a suit and tie, to see me. She also got Chalky to come over. They went over my version of what happened again. The inspector questioned me about other events and the treatment I'd witnessed to other boys. He wanted names and dates. The names I gave him, but the dates were a problem. One day was much like another. Also, since beatings were the norm, who got whacked on what day and for what reason was vague in my mind.

A week later, I met Ronnie, Bonker, and Kelly at the air-raid shelter. Ronnie had gotten cigarettes, ten Woodbines. They were giving smoking a try. Coughing and spluttering through our Woodbines, they told me about Mother. News had spread, but not about me—boys were always getting whacked—but this was different.

Mother had gone to the school. She walked into Bull-face's classroom, picked up his plimsole, and chased him out of the classroom, giving him several good whackings. Next she went into the headmaster's study, grabbed his cane, and chased him around the school hall. Finally, she broke the cane over her knee, opened his cupboard, and broke his entire cane collection. A sniveling boy waiting in Rottweiler's study got a reprieve.

I was taken aback—she had said nothing to me—but I was proud of Mum. Some justice had been achieved. It didn't help me much, but I felt good. Maybe Mother had saved other boys from a thrashing. I'd warned Bull-face about my Dad, but it never occurred to me to warn him about my mother.

I had no pity when I learnt three years later that Rottweiler had been sent to prison for cruelty and other vile acts to his charges. He was a man I was supposed to look up to. My god, how I despised him! Prison was too good for him. He should have been turned over to Kelly and his block and tackle.

The end of the war came abruptly. Even though we had anticipated it for weeks, the euphoria Winston Churchill's announcement produced was electrifying. "At 11:01 a.m., there will be a cessation of hostilities in Europe." It was VE Day, Victory in Europe, May 8, 1945. The war in Europe was over.

Buntings and flags appeared from nowhere. Church bells rang all day. Washing lines of red, white, and blue pennants strung across the roads and between lampposts. Old mattresses, blackout paper, and the innards of air-raid shelters made up a huge bonfire at the top of the estate. Trestles, tables, and chairs lined the streets. Merrymaking with music, dancing, and singing went on until the early hours of the morning. Parties—kids' parties, grown-up parties, and birthday parties, any excuse for a party—lasted for days.

Gradually, the jubilation and gratification subsided. The war was not yet over. We were still at war with Japan. The show wasn't going to be over until the fat lady sang, but in this case, it was going to be a fat boy.

Our soldiers didn't return either. They had other battles to fight. Our troops swarmed out of Europe after being deployed to Southeast Asia. Many British troops were already there, thousands were prisoners of war. Already the terror and horror of the Japanese concentration camps had reached our ears. We heard or read about torture, beheadings, starvation, and mass extermination. One after another horrific tale of Japanese atrocities unfolded. The overrun civilian population had fared no better. The Japanese vied with the Germans in abominable brutality.

After VE Day, the full impact of the horrors of German occupation exploded in the newspapers and at the cinema newsreels. The numbers meant little to me. One death I could mourn for. Ten deaths I could feel for. Twenty thousand or fifty million, the final count, were beyond my comprehension. Pictures appeared in the newspapers and in the footage of the newsreels—unbelievable pictures of the extermination and concentration camps of Buchenwald, Dachau, Belsen, Auschwitz, Chelmno, Belsec, and others. I saw pictures of thousands of corpses emaciated to stick figures, stacked like logs. The living dead stared blankly out of the newspapers. There were hundreds of thousands of the poor souls. What had they endured? With what memories? Could they ever really live again? There were mounds of spectacles, human hair, and baby shoes, the only evidence that millions of human beings had existed.

My exposure to the hideous scenes quickly reached saturation. I was numbed into watching without feeling. My emotions and mind couldn't accept more. Nightmare followed nightmare. Each one was the same. I was running down a corridor, stopping, German soldiers coming at me with fixed bayonets from both ends of the corridor. Then I awoke. To many, that scene had been their last nightmare.

There was a picture I related to. It startled me and brought back memories: a woman sorrowfully covered two children with a sheet. The children, fully dressed, were probably only five and six years old. The mother had shot them before the Russians closed in. It was a desperate act, a hopeless way of avoiding a fate worse than death. It made me shudder as I wondered if my mother had been thinking like that.

All eyes were on Japan. The question everybody had was "When is Japan going to surrender?" After an agonizing three months, the answer came. The fat boy sang. Two atomic bombs hit Japan: Little Boy on Hiroshima and, two days later, Fat Boy on Nagasaki. Weeks later, on September 2, the war was over. The newspapers and newsreels depicted the bomb's release, a ruthless force. Few people realized such power of destruction existed. The devastated areas were vast, an order of magnitude higher than anyone had seen on film before. In each case, one bomb created the devastation. Those people close to the blast were vaporized. Others half a mile away burned to death. Thousands more, at greater distances, died of internal hemorrhaging and bleeding.

The final terrifying fact that made people in the cinema gasp was the revelation that Hitler's scientists were only months away from perfecting their own atom bomb. England, no doubt, would have been one of the first test sites. Russia and the USA to follow. Another chilling thought.

We left the cinema after the newsreel, feeling numb. I couldn't stay for the main feature. Mother felt the same.

For me, the final realization that the war had truly ended didn't come until the second Sunday of November even though the sequences of news and events before then were happy ones. There were victory parades with tanks, military bands, and representations of all the Allied forces marching amidst bunting, flag waving, cheering, and parties.

Joe and Christine turned up with their baby daughter named after Mother. Chalky surprised us, visiting with his son who was the spitting image of his father. GranDad was busy in London, setting up a new home with a widow. Mum was pleased because it meant GranDad was on the mend, as she put it. Marvin came out of the hospital and planned to take Ronnie and his mother to America. Kelly's mother was planning to remarry. Bonker's dad returned from sea.

Dad came home in late October. For me, his return was the beginning of the end of the war. I was finding some peace, peace in my mind. I began to sleep well again with few nightmares. Peace was returning to my world.

The second Sunday in November was Remembrance Sunday. The town held a parade and church service. The whole estate emptied. People streamed over the common. The crowd swelled as we filed into town. This time, there was no profusion of Union Jacks and little bunting on display. Practically, everyone wore black armbands. It was the day peace finally came. Large clouds drifted by in a pale blue sky, and a watery sun peeped through, fitting the sober mood of the day.

Thirty thousand or more people filled the town. The market area either side of the clock tower was packed. The pavement held six or eight deep. Most people dressed in uniform or dark clothes. An amalgamation of Scots and Royal Marines bandsmen headed the parade. The bagpipes sounded magnificent, not brash marching music but softer lilting sounds that set the tone. I looked for Llewellyn. He could have been any one of the bandsmen. All the Allied armed services were represented: every auxiliary including the Merchant navy, fire service, home guard, women's, and other voluntary groups. It was a remembrance day for everyone. Spectators too. A service of songs and sermons led up to a two-minute silence, the time to coincide with the finish in Europe of both the First and Second World Wars.

As eleven o'clock drew near, the noise of the crowd edged into a silence. Nothing stirred. There was utter stillness. The clock tower boomed the hour. As the last strike of the chime faded away, a voice echoed through the loudspeakers:

They shall not grow old
As we are left to grow old.
Age shall not weary them,
Nor the years condemn.
At the going down of the sun
And in the morning,
We will remember them.

The crowd remained silent for two more minutes. Not a murmur. All were in deep thought, remembering. No one had been untouched by the war. A peal of trumpets broke the silence. "The Last Post," the final salute, reverberated around the town.

That was the day the war ended for me, during the harmony and tranquility of the remembrance service. Calmness and peace permeated my mind, my body, and my soul. I would be able to sleep soundly again. My future children and grandchildren would be able to live and sleep in peace.